Finding Our Voice

Finding Our Voice

Embodying the Prophetic
and Other Misadventures

MARC H. ELLIS

CASCADE *Books* • Eugene, Oregon

FINDING OUR VOICE
Embodying the Prophetic and Other Misadventures

Copyright © 2018 Marc H. Ellis. All rights reserved. Except for brief quotations in critical publications or reviews, no part of this book may be reproduced in any manner without prior written permission from the publisher. Write: Permissions, Wipf and Stock Publishers, 199 W. 8th Ave., Suite 3, Eugene, OR 97401.

Cascade Books
An Imprint of Wipf and Stock Publishers
199 W. 8th Ave., Suite 3
Eugene, OR 97401

www.wipfandstock.com

PAPERBACK ISBN: 978-1-4982-9678-6
HARDCOVER ISBN: 978-1-4982-9680-9
EBOOK ISBN: 978-1-4982-9679-3

Cataloguing-in-Publication data:

Names: Ellis, Marc H.

Title: Finding our voice : Embodying the prophetic and other misadventures / Marc H. Ellis.

Description: Eugene, OR: Cascade Books, 2018.

Identifiers: ISBN 978-1-4982-9678-6 (paperback) | ISBN 978-1-4982-9680-9 (hardcover) | ISBN 978-1-4982-9679-3 (ebook)

Subjects: LCSH: Judaism—Political aspects. | Jewish ethics. | Israel—Moral conditions.

Classification: DS119.76 E58 2018 (paperback) | DS119.76 (ebook)

Manufactured in the U.S.A.   06/18/18

To the memory of my father

God told Elijah: "Get out of here, and fast. Head east and hide at the Kerith Ravine on the other side of the Jordan River. You can drink fresh water from the brook; I've ordered the ravens to feed you."

The prophet is human, yet employs notes one octave too high for our ears. The prophet experiences moments that defy our understanding. The prophet is neither a "singing saint" nor a "moralizing poet," but an assaulter of the mind. Often the prophet's words begin to burn where conscience ends.

—Abraham Joshua Heschel

Judaism, disdaining this false eternity, has always wished to be a simultaneous engagement and disengagement. The most deeply committed person, the prophet, is also the most separate being, and the person least capable of becoming an institution.

—Emmanuel Levinas

Contents

Preface | ix

1 Finding Our Voice | 1
The Deepening Voice | 3
Where Our Heart First Moved | 4
Our Primal Witness | 5
Encountering Our Primal Prophetic Voice | 7

2 Prophetic Interiors | 11
Prophetic God-Wall | 14
Light Gatherers from Somewhere Else | 16
Married to the Prophetic | 19
Once in a Blue Moon Prophetic | 21

3 Negotiating the Prophetic | 28
Prophet-Sharing | 34
Prophetic Hope—Within Disaster | 38
The Persistence of the Prophetic | 42
Israel's Unstable God | 46
Dissident Israelis | 50
Prophetic Asceticism and the Destitute Other | 53

4 Our Prophetic Future | 62
   Jewish Prophetic Afterlife | 67
   Prophetic Remnants | 75
   Prophet Trauma/Prophet Mysticism | 83
   Prophet Confession | 92
   The Entangled Prophetic | 100
   Jewish Prophets in Decimated Gaza | 111

Epilogue | 123

Preface

In our personal lives the search for meaning is paramount. Yet meaning is often elusive. We are always one step ahead—or behind—the collapse of meaning.

Though we usually think of the meaning of life in relation to love and family, I believe the primary gateway to meaning is the prophetic.

The Bible, at least, is clear on this matter. Without the prophetic, the Bible loses focus. The center of the Bible disappears. Especially in the Hebrew Bible, the prophetic is omnipresent. Many years ago, the great Jewish theologian, Abraham Joshua Heschel, wrote that the Bible emphasizes God's pursuit of humanity. I believe the Bible has a more ominous subtext.

Throughout the Bible, humanity is shadowed by the prophetic. The prophetic call is everywhere in the Bible and communicated in diverse settings with distinct voices. What distinguishes the prophetic call from other themes in the Bible is that it resides at the center of our humanity. That is the positive side of the prophetic.

Unfortunately, the prophetic has a less savory side. The call to justice and compassion, even to the point of opposing the wayward drift of one's community, is dangerous to our physical and psychological health. The prophet's demand is too much to bear.

At the outset, the prophetic seems clear-cut. As we respond to the prophetic call, however, we recognize the prophetic has many aspects. What seemed at the outset to be straightforward becomes puzzling. The prophet experiences dissonance and discord. Immersed in a battle that has no end, the prophet is caught up short.

The prophet appears to be an unmovable object. Even the passage of time cannot efface the prophetic voice. Yet the interior of the prophet is vulnerable.

The prophet reaches for justice as a way toward meaning. In the prophet's mind, injustice unearths the human and divine abyss. Yet the prophet finds justice to be as elusive as meaning.

The distinction between the prophet and the prophetic is complex. Sometimes the two are intertwined. Other times they are distinct. The prophet is an individual; the prophetic usually signifies a movement. The biblical prophets are the progenitors of the prophets and prophetic movements of our time. Prophets and prophetic movements inherit a tradition.

Today, God cannot be called on to justify the prophetic voice. For too many, and for good reason, God's claims fall on deaf ears. Even the religious have doubts about God. The prophet/prophetic is on its own.

To what purpose the prophet? To what end the prophetic? As the contemporary explosion of the prophetic continues, in the Jewish community, for example in relation to Israel's oppression of Palestinians, and in the Christian community, through a now globalized series of liberation theologies, its failure is all the more obvious. We are left with a shattered prophetic carried by exiles of every stripe.

Exiles journey into the evolving prophetic community of our time. I call this communal gathering of prophetic exiles the New Diaspora.

I do not have the answer to the question of meaning that the prophet carries as his hallmark. In these pages, I share only a series of meditations, posed in purposely short, originally handwritten, paragraphs. They represent for me another attempt to come to grips with the failing, yet defining, prophetic at the center of our lives.

Preface

Since my thinking about the prophetic is ongoing, I originally limited my reflection to one hundred statements composed over a few intense and difficult days. This writing is found in the book's second chapter, "Prophetic Interiors." Some of these original statements have been further divided for easier reading. I think of these meditations as a prophetic snapshot, a moment in time when I committed to paper prophetic fragments that came my way.

Some of these statements are, no doubt, politically incorrect. Activist groups cannot mobilize around my understanding of the doomed prophet and prophetic movements that believe that the prophetic is only an activism oriented toward success. Mobilizing for justice has its place. Deeper reflection has its place as well. "Prophetic Interiors" is not an activist manual. These are meditations for the time before and after activity on behalf of justice.

As I wrote "Prophetic Interiors," I was simultaneously writing what became the first chapter and the title of my book, *Finding Our Voice*. This, too, is a meditation on the voice within us, how we locate it, and how it forms the essence of who we are. "Finding Our Voice" and "Prophetic Interiors" can be read separately, or one after the other. To my mind, the order matters little. Though the ground may be similar, the nuances are important. The prophetic is voice. The voice is prophetic.

Surviving and flourishing in life as individuals and communities is complicated. Thus, if we are honest, the prophetic is also negotiated. In the third and fourth chapters of the book, I explore the multilayered dimensions of the evolving prophetic, a prophetic with and without God and in a modernity that elevates the few and makes destitute the many. With the election of Donald Trump as President of the United States in 2016, the place of the prophetic became even more important.

Knowing that every system is flawed and unstable, does the prophetic seek to overturn the entire political system or operate on the margins of political change? The prophet is political in orientation or, rather, the prophet hones a spirituality that is near and distant from the urgent issues which confront us. For the twists and turns of the political order are fleeting, moving one way and

Preface

then another. Meanwhile, the world crisis deepens. The prophetic persists but is entangled. What are we to make of the entangled prophetic?

I offer my reflections on the prophets in the tradition of Abraham Joshua Heschel, who wrote his magisterial work on the prophets in Europe as Hitler and the Nazis consolidated power, and Emmanuel Levinas, the Lithuanian/French philosopher, who wrote so hauntingly about the prophets in the aftermath of World War II and the early years of the state of Israel. There is so much yet to learn from both. Yet we live in another time. Heschel's dire warnings about the triumph of evil and the need to hold fast to God and Levinas's desolate prophetic landscape and conflicted hope for the new Jewish state as a beacon to the world, remain with us. Yet, today, we must forge ahead. The Jewish prophets and the prophetic in general now come after the Holocaust, with so many genocidal events occurring since, and after Israel, with Israel's occupation and oppression of Palestinians and other oppressive forces around the world. The prophetic remains. The prophetic evolves.

In the Epilogue, I share my reflections on the long haul of the prophetic. What does the prophetic have to say to this crisis that becomes more obvious at times but really moves far beyond election cycles and international agreements? On the streets around the world, the outrage is palpable. What remains is a deeper reckoning.

We bequeath our search for meaning to our children. What they will make of our search is for them to explore and articulate. The marvel of marvels is that the persistence of the prophetic assures me that the thoughts found here will be extended and amended.

I wait eagerly for the next generation of the prophets. Indeed, they have already arrived.

1

Finding Our Voice

I found my voice early. Or did it find me? Perhaps my voice was already there, waiting. If my voice was already there, waiting, were the voices of others waiting, too? Are they still waiting?

Yes other voices are being found every day. My voice joins those who came before mine. Their voice joins mine. With other voices on the way. Strange how all our voices sound the same yet remain distinct. As if a common voice is already there waiting to be discovered and spoken. Exiled voices. Voices in the New Diaspora. Voices who claim God. Voices who don't. Loud voices. Voices that remain in the shadows. Does my voice, our voices, mean change is imminent, profound, revolutionary? Or does my voice, do our voices, mean that change will arrive in a time other than our own?

Our voices may be like the Christian belief in the Second Coming of Jesus. It is delayed so often that Christian hope is often prayed rote. Like the pledge of allegiance. One nation, under God. The question being whether our voices are for the change we want and need or if something else is occurring that as yet cannot be seen or named.

Finding Our Voice

I think of my son, Aaron, finding his voice. Some years ago wandering around a Bible-belt town wearing a sandwich board sign: GODISNOWHERE. When he asked me what his sign said, I responded: "God is nowhere." He corrected me. "Dad, it could mean "God is now here." A God Rorschach test I suppose. What you believe, you see. Yet another test for our voice, since by then I had already moved from what I initially saw in his sign. Without, however, arriving at his alternative destination.

So my son, Aaron, the eldest, and my little one, Isaiah, who isn't little anymore, are now finding their voices. Having grown up hearing my voice, can they trust the voice they find is their own? No one wants a borrowed voice to name our world. Yet to some extent our voices are borrowed, from the past, our family upbringing, culture, and religious heritage. Searching for a voice that has never been heard before is endless. Then how is it that voices as yet unheard, even if they have echoes of what has gone before, continue to appear and surprise us with their singularity?

When we hear a distinctive voice, we know it. As if out of nowhere, suddenly the voice is now here. The voice we have yet to hear startles us. We recognize its difference in the very first words spoken. Which, paradoxically, seems self-evident. Once spoken they seem to have been around forever.

We cannot get this voice out of our mind. From that moment on it shadows us as a clarion call. We are challenged to find our voice or to buckle down and recover the deeper timbre of the voice we found long ago.

The voice of the Other becomes part of our being; it never leaves us. Though distinct and compelling, it comes from a place we cannot identify. The sheer force of naming the heretofore unnamed confronts us with an invitation to search its origins. We are stymied. Even the explanation of where the voice is coming from—the person speaking or from God—is insufficient. In the end we have our limitations. We might conclude that the voice which stops us in our tracks and turns us around comes neither from an individual nor from God. Rather, it comes from Somewhere Else.

Finding Our Voice

THE DEEPENING VOICE

As I found my voice, I discovered an unexpected silence within me. At first, I couldn't explain it. This discovery forced a deeper exploration of my voice and self. In due time, I found the prophetic within, my life partner, through thick and thin. But then I asked if the prophetic, so bold and outspoken, could be rooted in silence. Even if this were the case, who in God's name could explain a seeming paradox, that those with bold public voices also dwell in the solitude we usually associate with a monk?

For those who find their voice early, the monkish quality of the prophetic is often a late discovery. Perhaps this is because the prophetic—at least in the world—doesn't go very far. After years of itinerant preaching of justice, the world remains the same. Or worse. Silence may be the fallback position for the discovered voice that lacks discernible effect in the world. Does this lack reduce the discovered and articulated voice to a silent plea? The plea, that despite all, humanity will survive the displacement and violence that is a foundational structure of history. Perhaps the silent plea was already there, forced to become articulate for a time, only to retreat to its origins in later years.

On the one hand, our voice, so ineffective even and especially when magnified on stage, reverberates in the ongoing public debate. On the other hand, our voice becomes part of the silence others will discover within themselves. Perhaps both, though how our voice persists beyond ourselves and within others is a mystery.

Persistence in a universe where disappearance and change is the coin of the realm is hard to explain. The persistence of the prophetic is especially difficult to chart. Such persistence cannot be ascribed to biology, as if there is a prophetic DNA strand indigenous to Jews but now, through Christianity and Islam, is available to all. Like the voice found in silence, the prophetic evolves. The prophetic essence remains.

Today, it is almost impossible to assert "essence," since cultural, political, religious and creative construction rather than persistence is emphasized. Demanded? But even if our voice—our silence—is constructed to a large extent across generations and manifold borders, there seems to be an essential place of mutual recognition. Which means that though changes in human context are certain, a basic foundation remains.

The dead ends of life. In politics, culture and religion. Outside of us. Within us, too. When we reach a dead end we feel it in our voice. What we speak no longer rings true. At first, we continue out of habit. The voice we found is the voice we have. Suspicion and fear lurks. If the voice we found is the voice we have, and is now inadequate, can we afford to let our voice go silent? There may not be another voice waiting in the wings.

So the voice we discover, the voice that comes within silence, coming from Somewhere Else, is not our only voice or our deepest voice. The voice we have at any given moment is the voice we have at that moment. This hardly makes our voice relative simply because it changes with age and context. Rather it means that our voice is constantly *en route*, surfacing here and there, then retreating, sometimes almost dying when, surprise, surprise, our voice returns changed and new.

WHERE OUR HEART FIRST MOVED

The persistence of the voice. Like the prophetic, our voice remains. What triggers the renewed voice, with words we haven't heard before or arranged in a somewhat different way, is another mystery. At times our voice surges ahead. Suddenly, our voice changes. Other times our voice retreats, if only to recover themes we thought lost. It takes a long time to return to our origins. Where our heart first moved.

When you think your voice is needed all the time, when you think your voice is the only voice, that the world cannot go on without hearing from you, it is time to be silent. Watch and see if the world continues on its way. Of course, here is the very problem for the voice that speaks truth to power. Whatever the truth of the matter, the world continues with or without us.

Finding Our Voice

Our voice sounds the alarm. Something is wrong. We must alter course. Once altered, we reach safe harbor, so it seems. Is our voice, then, about hope? Yet, often and almost always, the alarm isn't heard. Worse still, the alarm is heard and little is done about the perilous situation we have uncovered. Our voice turns. Despair becomes our voice's timbre. What to do with the voice of hope that knows despair is the order of the day? Because if your voice has been around the block, it knows well the silence of deaf ears.

The unheard voice is much like the voice that is heard. The results are mostly the same. Self-interest and power wins the day, all the way down society's food chain. The voice of conscience interrupts this food chain and spreads panic near and far. If this voice is heard and acted upon where will it lead? Conscience is ordered anarchy; it leaves no stone unturned. So, too, the voice that refuses to be silenced.

The voice used to pass the time. We have little else to do. The rote voice—for us—still has the ability to move others who are searching for their voice. Our sequence is ours alone. Is the role of the teacher, for example, or the preacher, priest or rabbi, to continue on regardless until others hear our voice in theirs?

A reckoning occurs. Serving others is one thing. When your voice is involved, however, serving others can only be a secondary effect. When you involve your voice in serving others, it becomes too reverential, cautious, with this and that boundary a role model fastidiously adheres to.

The danger is clear. When your voice becomes a platitude even those you serve observe it as fake.

OUR PRIMAL WITNESS

Our lives are surrounded by secrets and lies. This encourages a silence that disciplines the voice. For speaking out a in world full of secrets and lies is dangerous. Our livelihood, even our physical being, is on the line.

Secrets and lies do more than threaten. They distort our voice. Our voice becomes something it isn't. Political correctness can do the same. Transparency is often another subterfuge. Secrets and lies are rarely confined to the political side we disrespect. In a corrupt world the voice enters another level of struggle.

Why speak when corruption wins the day?

We speak in a world full of secrets and lies because something is at stake in history. Though our voice seems directed at the issues of our day, there are other, usually unannounced arenas. What does it mean to be Christian, Muslim, Black, Filipino, South African? If our voice comes from Somewhere Else, it is likewise deeply rooted in the history of a people's struggle. Think of this as our primal geography, the place we can locate. Here, the compliment to Somewhere Else.

Our primal geography, the Somewhere Else on earth, where we come from, the particularity that grounds us, the history of struggle and contribution, is now at stake. Our voice has been honed there, now here. Our primal geography shapes our voice but, like that Somewhere Else, though more definable, a mystery remains. At the center of Jewishness or Blackness is a mystery we try to name. Often it is named by others. Our lifelong struggle begins. What is our primal witness in the world?

Yes, primal, as in essence, the voice originated long ago. Which doesn't mean a too easy repetition. The primal voice, always old, is, at the same time, always unfolding.

The primal voice is an anachronism, a relic of something deep and abiding. The primal voice becomes our primal voice. By becoming our voice, the seeming outdated holdover surprises the new with depth and calls it to account. Yet it could hardly hold the present to account if the primal voice wasn't within and responding to the present moment.

The primal voice has its own cadence and performs in public. Coming from a primal geography, as a response to the other performances of religious and political power, the curtain rises.

So far, so good. The ancient and contemporary primal voice speaks. The primal voice comes out of silence, the closest we come to naming that elusive Somewhere Else. The primal voice speaks its word and, too often, suffers the consequences. The primal voice is hit by the powers that be and, as second blow, the prospect of failure.

There is a third factor. The primal voice is always contested, especially in the community from which it springs. Think of the contestation within Jewish life. Already in the Bible you see two sides of Israel's primal voice. One side embraces the prophetic as Israel's destiny. The other sees Israel's destiny as empire. The division between the prophetic and empire run through Jewish history. It produces internal Jewish civil wars that last into the present. Every community has a similar struggle. Thus quiet on the community identity front is rare. The contestation is ongoing. Which primal voice, the prophetic or empire, will win the day?

ENCOUNTERING OUR PRIMAL PROPHETIC VOICE

An early reviewer of Samuel Beckett's plays called Beckett the "grammarian of solitude." Beckett captured the cadence of solitude. Or did the reviewer proffer Beckett as a writer who made solitude articulate? Perhaps both.

Is it possible to be a grammarian of the voice, primal, prophetic and otherwise? To what end? It could be that the primal prophetic voice is enough. Why study a subject whose origin can only be alluded to and the performance of which has to be encountered to be believed?

Encountering the prophetic voice is to feel its force, ancient cadence, and contemporary relevance. When you encounter the prophetic voice you sense being in time and out of time, and that the voice you hear is already too late and, paradoxically, right on time.

Encountering the prophetic voice is more than study or writing about the voice so difficult to define. Encountering this voice is its own event. It cascades forward and backward, being at another place within our own geography while creating its own terrain we then inhabit.

The primal prophetic voice is a geography unto itself. It leads us Somewhere Else and into the world, too.

The grammarian of solitude and the grammarian of the primal prophetic voice are similar. They may be two sides of the same coin. Same side? However the point of solitude and the voice isn't, in the first place, study. Nor is it amplification.

Critical appreciation of the primal prophetic voice is fine as long as its performance isn't handed over to those who desire to discipline or erase the encounter that turns the world inside out. Turning the world inside out shouldn't be handed over to employed academics or clerics whose job it is to build and maintain their careers. For these interpreters too often seek to make the primal prophetic voice their own, devoid of risk and mystery.

The primal prophetic voice is a mystery on many levels. with its persistence, endurance, old age, newness, its ability to encompass all of these seeming disjunctions at the same time. How to sum up the primal prophetic? And, of course, its randomness. We never know when and where the primal prophetic voice will appear, when it will subside or when it will come again.

The primal prophetic voice is like a wild card that we know is in the deck but don't know when it will be drawn. Nor do we know its effect in advance.

Wild cards can remain in the deck until the game is over. They can be drawn to little effect or seal the deal. Throughout the game we anticipate them being drawn for or against our interest. The wild card shadows ordinary play. The anticipation is real. But if one wild card does not seal the deal, the game goes on. We wait for the other wild card to be drawn.

Are we ashamed of our primal voice, especially when it is prophetic? The intellectual currents, in the West at least, look askance at the primal. Or romanticize it. Today our particular identities are submerged, or at least they are supposed to be. The primal causes division and strife. Better the universal voice—freedom and equality for all.

Yet our voice—primal, prophetic, or otherwise—is hardly universal. Our empire voice, whose mission is ostensibly universal,

Finding Our Voice

isn't universal either. Our history and context shape us. They are the foundations from which we move in the world. In the world our history and context continue to shape us and our voice. Do they also limit us?

Borders exist in life and voice. Yet the limits they impose are flexible. Limitations and boundaries can imprison us. Our constraints can also embolden and expand our view of ourselves and the world. Our voice carries the primal and the prophetic bound in the particular. Being bound, we become free. At least, struggle to be free.

For our primal prophetic voice is rarely determined in advance. Within the tension of past and present our voice takes shape. Our voice becomes serious through engagement. Disappointment, too.

Our primal prophetic voice carries empire within it. Somewhere near or far historically, empire is there. The desire to be on top, to dominate, to be served, to have privilege above others. The contest between community and empire is found within our voice. Temptations abound. Our primal prophetic voice struggles with its empire leanings.

For if we truly want the justice we speak of, surely we seek to subjugate the powerful once and forever. To do this, force is required, a force that is institutionalized and surrounded by symbols that make clear the battle for justice has been waged and won. The triumphant justice voice has too often turned into the very voice it once overturned. The prophetic as empire is cautionary.

Finding our primal prophetic leads to exile. This is true both in the larger world and in the particular world we come from. Our voice faces another challenge. It is difficult enough to find our voice in the first place. Exiled for speaking our word, our voice is tested. Do we have the fortitude to carry on when the price of finding our voice is compounded by the violence we experience?

Our primal prophetic voice is experienced as a form of violence against the powers that be. Our voice is a violation of right order—as defined by empire. Thus the force used to silence our voice. Yet the violence of the powerful is disproportionate. Most often the primal prophetic voice has little more than the voice itself. So why are the powerful so worried?

2

Prophetic Interiors

All of us know that the exile is here to stay. Exiles aren't going anywhere, if the truth be known.

Thus the challenge. Exile without community. Exile with community. What to do with the diversity of exilic life when the trauma of exile is so devastating. Ongoing. Never to be healed, if we are honest with ourselves and each other.

No one identity will suffice to encompass the prophetic today. Identities won't do the job either. The multiple identities movement carries a partial truth. We cannot stand firm and be faithful simply by being open and for others. The prophetic is neither open nor closed—only.

We are deprived, true. We are on the run, yes. We cannot call on God, as if God will intervene, just like that. Or protect us when we are in need. The biblical Elijah, being fed by ravens, is not for us. No chariots in the whirlwind either.

The prophetic is weak. The prophetic is on its own. Once given in biblical times, the prophetic is now free to land where it lands. The prophetic dances to its own music.

Yet the prophetic is spare change. Transformation is slow. One step forward, two steps back or more, it seems.

Does the prophetic matter? The world continues on. As does betrayal. The trauma deepens. The prophetic is itself a trauma. What to do with these traumas. Our abiding question.

The prophetic is a question—without an answer. The only thing we can do with the prophetic is to embody it. Without a sense of going anywhere. Just live it. Because we have little choice.

Was it always this way? The biblical prophets may have been on their own—really. The prophets may have imagined a calling from God—in their minds. We may be imagining that God is absent, faraway—only. Silent God. Could be. Perhaps.

No Choice Prophets, no promise of salvation, no recourse, no rescue. Don't tell the prophets it will be better in heaven than it is on earth. No prophet pie in the sky. No answer as to why either. The prophetic is like a prison where we find our difficult freedom.

With no answer to the God question, why bother? Those who know the answer either way know little. Does it matter in the end? Fidelity is being present in the way we can be present. Where we are, in our time. The rest is beyond us.

So if we embody the prophetic. Making whatever claims we have to, or no claims. In the New Diaspora, where the community of exiles resides, we chat about what makes us tick. When we want to, without having to worship at someone else's altar. Simple as that. But, then, nothing is simple in life. Our altars are complicated. Entangled.

The prophetic is disturbing, an ordeal, trauma. Always has been. Trauma is never simple, nor is sacrifice on behalf of others. When we refuse self-interest as the center of our lives, we enter a precarious landscape. We become part of an ancient and quite peculiar tradition.

How do we account for the origins and persistence of the prophetic? The persistence of the prophetic takes prophetic origins a step further. Then becomes now. Now becomes then.

The persistence of the prophetic augurs something within and beyond the humanity we usually experience. In the prophetic

Prophetic Interiors

journey we confront the essence of individuals and humanity at large. What is left of the earth and civilization after our experience of hope and betrayal is the lesson of lessons.

The thunder of the prophets startles us. After the thunder, the prophetic becomes less dramatic and more interesting. The wounds of those who have stared history in the face are upsetting. The prophet is humbled. We turn away. The prophetic remains. We turn toward.

The defeated prophets—vanishing. The defeated prophets—reappearing. The defeated prophets—persisting. The defeated prophets—remembered. The defeated prophets—humanity's wild card?

Which is more profound, the subversive memory of suffering or the subversive memory of the prophets? Perhaps they are one and the same.

The prophet wants more than defeat, of course, but even the prophet's victories are shadowed by defeats to come. Shadowed, too, by the prophets to come. Since there is no end to the suffering in history, or the prophets.

Hope chastened by what lies ahead. Then the question of questions. Gratitude for the exile prophetic that is defeated, one that carries a hope without hope, until the end?

The prophetic journey becomes more dangerous. The prophet is abandoned. There's empire power around every corner. Without being able to claim God, success, or hope, the prophetic is stripped naked, yet soldiers on.

Against the wall, the prophetic might be drawn to Samuel Beckett's despair. Sign up for the Amen Choir. Or continue on. There is no other road to travel. In the New Diaspora, exiles have each other. Barely enough on good days.

Even the New Diaspora is bursting with self-interest and careerists. The accolades and hugs the prophet experiences at the altar are mostly symbolic. Everyone's survival comes first. To think that the prophet will be offered real hospitality is an illusion. Prophets are lone wolf wild cards. The prophets are on their own.

We bequeath the prophetic to our children. What should we tell our children who embody the prophetic? To give themselves over to what has chosen them? Prophetic inheritances are difficult to hand down—and survive.

Knowing that the prophets are without a place to hide, with no ravens to feed them, surrounded by good people who cower before power, at least the power that might force them, once again, on the run. Such an inheritance is deeply ambivalent. Is bequeathing our prophetic inheritance irresponsible?

PROPHETIC GOD-WALL

As the prophet is lauded, others remain afraid. Lest they fall off the Empire Wheel they benefit from. The fear is natural. It also closes down thought. This is why our universities are "no thought" zones. More or less.

Progressive Christian seminaries are better, marginally, but the thought police, administrators and donors, have arrived there as well. As well, the seminary coffers are depleted. The long-running Christian empire is ending. So where will committed thought survive and flourish?

Fear spreads like a virus, until we forget where the fear began. We become stuck with New Age spirituality, progressive apocalyptic archetypes, and justice tourism. When you are on the ropes, expect the calls of support to come in the dead of night. If you are lucky.

In the dead of night. Dark corridors. Fleeting glances. Superficial statements: "Hope you are doing well." The prophet's supporters are closeted.

Our closets are full and overflowing, even as openness is celebrated. Mandated. How false! New power deals replacing the old power deals. Everywhere.

Daniel Berrigan, the late, radical Roman Catholic priest, once told me: "Walk with your fear." I did. Others have. Most don't. Walking with our fear is less about losing fear than channeling

Prophetic Interiors

it—somewhere. Still, positive outcomes are few and far between. There is always another fear-laden step to be taken.

The prophets are alone as they journey. As in ancient times. The prophets know solitary confinement like the back of their hand. The sound of doors closing behind them is familiar.

Walking with our fear. Alone. We find others walking with their fear. Alone. The community of prophets, the New Diaspora, is alone together.

The difficult balance. Solitude and solidarity define our lives. Art and poetry come from this tension. Our words about God come from there. As poetic hope. Not less. Not more.

God-talk as poetic hope. The prophetic as embodied poetic hope. On the edge of despair. Attempting to pry open the possibility of meaning in our lives and world, the prophets are surrounded by religions, large and small. For the prophet, though, religion is theatre. Kitsch. Where the prophet dies a lauded, noble death.

Religion disciplines the prophetic. Dressing up for God! The prophetic strips and stands naked before a meaningless world. On the threshold of meaning.

Without the prophetic there is no meaning in our lives. There may be no meaning in our lives. The prophet embodies the possibility of meaning in our lives. In history?

The prophet embodies the—possibility—of God. Much more than prayer. Is the prophet embodied prayer?

On the threshold of meaning. In history. Of God. Like love and beauty, always *en route*. Starting over each day. Without knowing where the prophetic will take us. Prophetic destination. Unknown.

You don't wake up one morning and find the prophetic gone. The prophetic isn't like that. The prophetic is given, engraved inside of you, or it isn't. You can't give the prophetic back to God. There isn't a shelf to put the prophetic on so you can try something else on for size.

How to say this in a world where an engraved essence seems absurd? Certain people are born with the prophetic. Stuck with it. For life. Because they are. No other reason need apply.

You ask yourself, especially when people ask you. Otherwise, it goes without saying. You are what you are. From the beginning. Then the road becomes difficult. Assaults come from all sides: "Who do you think you are!"

As if the prophets are introspective. As if the prophetic comes from "I." As if the prophet knows why what is, is.

The prophet deflects origins. Doesn't know them anyway. The interior of the prophet is like someone hitting her head against a wall. Is that wall, God?

God is too conceptual for the prophet. Nowadays. Whether God is or is not is hardly the point. The prophet isn't out to prove God or no-God. A waste of time! Let the clerics, with their liturgical incantations, direct that show.

LIGHT GATHERERS FROM SOMEWHERE ELSE

Performing religion. Performing the prophetic. Joined at the hip or pulling against each other? Either/or? Giving way to the prophetic, religion has its place. Still, the prophetic has no time for its nemesis. The prophet imagines no religion.

When the prophet hears "liturgy," he thinks "death." The incense is too much at religion's High Noon altar. As if any God worth her salt wouldn't think the same. Imagine God desiring worship in an unredeemed world. Scandal!

Laugh or cry, the absurdity of parts of life leaves us little choice. Even the notion that the prophetic is given, it's just there. Within some. Unearned. Not acquired. Consequences unknown. Absurd!

Sure, the prophetic can be learned and practiced up to a point. Nonetheless, the difference between the prophetic as given and learned is hard to dismiss. Or explain.

The prophet is a one-off character, appearing now and then. Known widely. Known in small circles. Hidden.

The prophetic is unusual, too, but more available. The prophetic is easier to discern and tolerate. The prophet moves deep into history. Into that darkness.

Prophetic Interiors

Speaking of these distinctions today is almost impossible. Politically and religiously incorrect. The poverty of our age illumined. Notions of equality make it impossible to speak of the prophet and the prophetic with any bite outside of social action. As if social action and equal voice is the abiding essence of the prophetic. As if action is all there is, sufficient, God-like. As if action is meaning itself. The truth of the prophetic is there and more. Much more.

Movements come and go. Like rain, movements are happening somewhere, always. The deeper grasp, that entry into history, the ability to see suffering and hope, to gather light in the darkness. To hold it all together. This is the prophet's task.

Gathering light. Light gatherers. The prophetic, too. But the prophet is on a different level. This should be celebrated. Sometimes is. Most often in retrospect.

Gathering light—the prophets. In the darkness. Not from it. Not to announce light, which is too easy. Just seeing glimpses. Witnessing to the possibility of light. Horizon light.

The end the prophet knows isn't the end. Without the prophet knowing the end either. Prophetic glimpses. Even when victory seems to be right around the corner. Of the dark days stretching out ahead.

Gathering light, the prophet and the prophetic are stripped bare. Shattered. Only prophetic fragments remain. Prophetic fragments don't add up to much. Nonetheless, there is an explosion of the prophetic in our time. Hardly makes sense. At first light.

Has the prophetic ever made sense? We read the Bible as if the Bible makes sense. Does it? The Bible is constructed, fashioned, to become an unfolding story. Which it isn't, really.

The Bible is what was made of it. What we make of it. What a hold it has over us! For good reason. For many, the Bible is a place to stand. With feet planted. From which we move.

Martin Buber, the great Jewish scholar, believed the most important figures in the Bible were failures. Especially the prophets. Buber believed those failures accumulate through history, paradoxically, creating the pathway for redemption.

The reversal of reversals. Failure equals redemption. A secret history. Known by the prophets. Is Buber right?

The prophets are agnostic on redemption through failure. What other option/belief is available? Viable?

Failure. Redemption. There has to be more to the prophetic. Success as the world knows it is less than advertised. Worldly success is far from redemption. Is worldly, itself, failure? We need worldly success. Yet it seems that such success, or the search for it, almost always dumbs things down. Thought is dumbed down. Action, too.

The prophetic needs to be engaged. It also needs distance. The prophet mines the darkness. The light she finds, for the most part, isn't going anywhere.

The prophet witnesses suffering and experiences his own. The prophet wants suffering to end and knows it will continue. If suffering does end here it will be recycled and appear elsewhere. This doesn't mean the prophet dwells in apathy or cynicism. It means the prophet is digging deeper, determined to go the last, most difficult, mile.

The last mile means everything. The Last Mile Prophetic. Another mystery that begs the prophet question. Do you doubt there is an answer? Still, when we experience a prophetic presence we know it. We enter another space. That space is more than success or failure.

The prophet and the prophetic moment come from another place, a place we cannot identify or define. It isn't otherworldly. It's not from God. Not from us. It isn't from here or there. The prophet and prophetic must be from Somewhere Else.

Somewhere Else is defined in different ways at different times. In our time we lack the ability to name Somewhere Else. This hardly means that Somewhere Else is just our imagination playing tricks when our so-sophisticated modern mind-games fail us.

Modern mind-games are similar to the endless deconstruction of the Bible. Over time it becomes a vocation with tenure and reasonable pay. As if what takes the Bible's place is so much better.

Modernity's Bible isn't doing so well after all. Even deconstructing God—eternally!—has its rewards and limits. There are all sorts of Gods out there. Endless number.

MARRIED TO THE PROPHETIC

The prophets should be held accountable. In the Bible, the prophets are way too strong. Too judgmental. Too temperamental. Too dependent on God.

The prophet's call comes from Somewhere Else, true, but the prophet's insistence is unbearable. Our Too Much Prophets need a talking to. Let the discussion begin.

If you have ever wrestled with a prophet, assume you are wrestling with yourself. Forget that you are unworthy. Thinking yourself unworthy is a convenient excuse for dodging the prophetic bullet. Even when you have (temporarily) dodged the prophetic bullet, look over your shoulder. The prophetic is gaining on you.

We spend most of our lives looking over our shoulder. One thing or another—bills, jobs, criticism, relationships. What remains is the meaning of life. The answer is elusive. The prophetic comes into play here but most of the time we are distracted. We do not want what we cannot handle. The prophetic is trouble. The prophetic is also our last chance.

The Last Chance Prophetic. That old wild card again. When everything quiets down we are alone with our destiny. Who we are called to be.

Life can't be just doing this and that forever. Our heartbeat isn't—only—doing. Or being for others. Something is calling us from deep inside. We have difficulty facing this calling. We can't shake it either.

Thinking about the Last Chance Prophetic, did you hear the prophet of prophets, Noam Chomsky, the Jewish political thinker, speaking about the love he found—at eighty-five years of age? The great articulator on every political issue in our globalized world was caught up short when asked about his new found love. He had only clichés to offer. About the emptiness of life without love. How his lover, now wife, just "fell" into his arms!

The prophet in love. Life on the run is far from ideal. The personal side of life is diminished. Assimilated? The prophet is married to the prophetic. A marriage made in heaven, so to speak. Rather a marriage made Somewhere Else.

Since the prophet does not choose the prophetic, divorce is off the table. The idea of divorcing the prophetic is ridiculous. Forget it.

Even as the prophet is shown the door, refused meals or directed to the kitchen to eat—backdoor entrances aren't reserved for Negroes of the Old South—the marriage remains intact. And this when the Jewish prophetic remains the third rail in our modern times. Everywhere. Once again the persistence of the (indigenous) Jewish prophetic challenges our definitions. And our imagination.

The prophetic as the third rail of our globalized world. Though the prophetic's global impact comes through Christianity and Islam, it remains home-brewed Jewish. In our day, the Jewish prophetic has returned home as fierce and unrelenting as ever. Can Jews permanently oppress the Palestinian people without provoking a Jewish prophetic insurgency?

Returning home after a century or two of being on the global prowl, what does the Jewish prophetic find? Devastation. Ruin. Inconsolable, the prophet cries out. Empire Jews turn the screws tighter. Empire Jews seek to destroy him.

Strange to say, yet so instructive, in a world which now welcomes Jews, the Jewish prophetic has nowhere to hide. Empire Jewish power is around every corner. Christians who universalize their justice concerns resent Empire Jewish power. For the most part, they remain silent, tossing a symbolic bone of opposition now and then. Yet their silence is a reflection on their own limitations. Christians who are for justice in every corner of the globe bow to Empire Jewish power. For their own self-interest.

Corruption is everywhere. Original sin? Or is the timid Left simply securing its own survival? To what purpose? For the bigger, more important issues, no doubt. Or the issues which once

Prophetic Interiors

were the third rail and are no longer. Impersonating Prophets. Fake-news.

Impersonating Prophets complicate the prophetic terrain. As if the terrain wasn't complicated enough. Some Christians are prophetic, yes, but for the Jewish prophets they are mostly absent. Even though prophetic Christians draw their strength from the tradition these contemporary Jewish prophets embody. Used and discarded, honored and betrayed, the Jewish prophetic inhabits a conflicted religious landscape.

The Jewish prophetic reaches out. Into an illusory common vineyard. The Jewish prophetic is expropriated by others. Without real Jews being present.

Is the Jewish prophetic without real Jews, real? The Jewish prophetic with only imaginary, often textual biblical Jews, present? Imagine that!

Prophetic farce? Compromised prophetic? Corrupted prophetic? Complicated prophetic. Negotiated prophetic. You wouldn't think the prophetic could be all of the above and nonetheless survive. It is. The prophetic survives.

Resilient Prophetic. The prophetic survives those who claim it. The prophetic survives itself.

The prophetic is far from easy, any way you shape or misshape it. Even the prophetic tradition has to be shaken. Every so often the prophetic has to take itself back. The prophetic has to be reclaimed in every generation.

The prophet poses, sometimes. The prophet screws up, sometimes. The prophet wants to retreat, sometimes. In the end, though, you know the prophet by when she stands up. At the most difficult moment. And keeps standing after the crowd has left the scene. That's the prophet.

ONCE IN A BLUE MOON PROPHETIC

During my morning prayers, I fix my gaze and remember a headline story. Of one who was driven out of town by a "Christian" who defends a wealthy businessman convicted of sex trafficking of underage girls and, later, more, much more. To earn big bucks? Cashing in. While making the sign of the Cross. An old story.

Defending sex traffickers for cash. Bowing your head in prayer. Those who remain silent. Bowing their heads in prayer. Seeing it all. Amazing stuff!

The cash we take and the silence we fake, all for the greater good. Of? There's a bigger story here. Much bigger. Always is.

Despite the corruption, the prophet refuses original sin. This is the prophetic bottom line. It is more important than the contested issue of God. Here's the deal: Original sin lets everyone off the hook, even God.

Accepting original sin and, worse, promulgating it, makes the prophet's journey even lonelier. While not everyone is a prophet, everyone is called to the prophetic. Original sin strikes the prophetic at its core. If humanity is unable to return to the right track, the right track being the place where we begin, who can the prophet address?

The prophet believes humanity has veered off course and that righting the direction is possible. Yet the difficult road ahead is obvious. It is as difficult as the road stretching out behind us. History is full of brutality. Holding to the belief that there is another way is hard.

The alternative? Not much to choose from. If the prophet says "yes" to original sin, humanity goes on its wayward path, with a religious blessing. If the prophet gives up on humanity's goodness, the abyss opens wide. Too wide.

The prophetic abyss. Ancient musings. You have to experience the lay of the land before you announce the apocalypse. What to do with what you find? Because the apocalyptic prophet rivals the abyss itself. The prophet has to see through and around the abyss. Without knowing if humanity can pull through.

Announcing the abyss as our future is anti-human. Though "human" is flexible, as we have seen in history, as we see now. Still, the prophet is hardly whistling in the dark about humanity. The prophet knows what's going on. The prophet and the prophetic gain a foothold in the abyss they struggle against.

Prophetic Interiors

The prophet refuses to be an abyss voyeur. The abyss is too dark for voyeurism. Even the light gathered there is surrounded by darkness.

While the prophet is unable to climb out of the abyss and knows that the abyss cannot be transcended, the prophet's abyss warning lights flash red. Imagine the prophet as a flashing red light guarding the abyss. So, too, the prophetic.

The prophet/prophetic rarely solves anything. That is the mistake made by those who want more from the prophetic than it can deliver. Solving the various economic, political, and ecological puzzles is above the prophet's pay grade. Whatever the solutions may be, they will be negotiated over time, way too slowly and with victims galore. As is always the case.

The prophet/prophetic isn't giving up on solutions. It's just that the prophet is driving on History Lane. Change in history is long and arduous. Revolutions do less than advertised. The future of peace and justice is mostly an illusion. "We Shall Overcome" should be retired.

The usefulness of the prophet is limited. The prophetic pushes the boundaries and opens possibilities for a future beyond the present. The prophetic banner is hope for the future. Still, the prophet is rarely about the future. The prophet is doomed. The prophet is about enslaved ancestors.

Asceticism is far from popular today. The prophet embraces asceticism like the training of a fighter.

Is the prophet a monk? More or less. Their solitude is similar. Unlike the monk, though, the prophet is constantly being knocked down and around by history's contestations. The mat the prophet lifts himself off of is miles away from the monk's hermitage. As conventionally understood.

The prophet's monastery is the world. The prophet monk is immersed in the everyday but at a distance. In the public eye, deep in exile, hidden away, the prophet monk is buried and forgotten. Once in a while the prophet reappears, disappears again and fades into obscurity.

The prophet's liturgy is vigilance. The prophet constantly fights the demons of despair. The prophet's field of battle is the world and the no-hope hope that envelops him.

Prophetic sutras. The non-canonical type. As in a collection of aphorisms in the form of a manual. A thread that hold things together. "Sutra"—Sanskrit, to sew.

The prophet as a seamstress. Searching for that worldly justice and compassion thread out in the world that prophet has discovered within. The prophet wonders why that thread within her is so hard to find in the world.

Like texts written on palm leaves and sewn together, the prophet leaves a legacy. Coming from long ago. Engaged in the future. To what effect? For whom?

A fascinating case in point. Will the Jewish prophets of our time, Jews of Conscience, be remembered within the Jewish fold? Doubtful. Will they be remembered in the gathering of exiles from around the world in the New Diaspora? More likely.

In the New Diaspora will Jews of Conscience be remembered as Jews who didn't arrive unexpectedly? Who embodied the Jewish indigenous? I wonder. Or will the Jewish prophets of our time be remembered simply as the prophetic salt of the earth who, like everyone else in the New Diaspora, went the extra mile in another's shoes?

It may be unimportant that Jews who come from the tradition that gave the prophetic to the world are remembered. It may be a vestige of Jewish self-interest, that chosenness thing that so upsets modern universalizers. On the other hand, remembering the Jewish prophetic through the Jewish prophets of our day may be the key to unlock other subversive traditions being lost to the world. A thought to ponder for Jews and non-Jews alike.

The Archaic Prophetic. Fancy that! As an embodied vision from the past that keeps reappearing to focus our attention. Since we banish the ancient, often for good reason, we hold up the modern, often for the worst of reasons. Like the prophetic, the modern needs to be humbled. Unlike the prophetic, if humbled, what would the modern have left to say?

Prophetic Interiors

Archaic layering. Not for old time's sake. The prophetic tradition is evolving right before our eyes. God is no longer at the center. Punishment for sins is left to right-wing televangelists. The prophetic won't be televised.

Stripped down, naked and unadorned, the prophet stands at modernity's abyss without easy answers. No Answer Prophets. Remaining at their post.

Steadfast. Still performing the prophetic. Without incense. The most ancient of rituals. With age, though, moving deeper into a solitude that solidarity cannot erase or minimize. Young, the world is moving. Is youthful movement a mirage?

Perhaps there are stages. What wasn't a mirage then, now is. Or what now seems to be a mirage is taken up, pushed forward by a new generation of prophetic Sisyphus's. Their boulder at the foot of the hill is more than an absurd happiness.

Aging prophets should look ahead rather than backward. Encouraging the next generation rather than lamenting the failures of her own.

What to say to those prophetic voices just embarking on the journey? Mirage-talk is unhelpful. Still, the prophet needs to encourage others when her chips are down. The wisdom the prophets have collected, the witness the prophets have lived, should be shared willingly. Without charge.

Sharing the prophetic is a challenge. As night falls.

Better silence? Half-truths? Especially your children. Look them in the eye. Tell them that the night falling now is the night falling for them, too. Tell them of the abyss the prophet knows well. Of the no-go areas that proliferate.

Regardless, our last prophetic breath has to be that a breakthrough is possible.

Be honest, though. Breakthrough is not going to happen, as in once-and-for-all. Breakthroughs are limited. They do happen. Once in a blue moon.

Blue moons should be celebrated. More blue moons may soon appear. Of course, the blue moon isn't blue. Blue moons occur when volcanic eruptions or exceptionally large fires leave debris particles in the air. Blue moons are a wonderful illusions we witness with our own eyes.

Blue moons, like the prophetic, are an angle of vision. There are large amounts of atmospheric debris in our traditions and the modern air we breathe.

The prophetic wild card remains somewhere in humanity's deck. It could show up at any blue moon moment. If we see a blue moon prophetic moment with our own eyes is it still a mirage or a truth dressed in a multi-colored robe?

So often the prophetic hides or comes too late. Or is so weak it cannot turn the tide or even register in the casino's take. To the powerful, the prophetic is chump change. Does that make the prophetic a mirage?

Only if existence is a mirage. Existence is the issue at hand, since we are all here one day and gone the next. The prophet is hardly exempt. No extra earthly or heavenly brownie points for prophetic witness either. Here one day, gone the next, is the fate of the prophets, too. Except in memory, though few are remembered by name.

If only the prophet's names were called out one by one every day of the year. Even if recalled by name, few would recognize them. The unknown prophets suffer, only to be buried in memory. Perhaps a worse fate befalls the known. They endure the ignominy of statues and national holidays in their name.

Long after the powerful have their way with the known prophets, power has its way with them again. The doomed prophets in life are trivialized in memory. Think Martin Luther King Jr., and the national holiday that honors him.

A prophet looks backward down history's long corridor. Being on time is essential for the prophet, but a look back shows the prophet's limits. Still, the prophet's witness is hardly time-bound.

The prophet/prophetic lives in time and out of time. The disconnect is obvious but difficult to wrap our minds around. Time-warp Prophetic. Another lesson for the prophetic.

Lessons are endless. Teachings are limited. The winner? Every life has its set of lessons and teachings. For the prophet, proportionality should not determine the final result. Otherwise the loss ledger leads. Becomes defining. Hands down.

Those moments when the prophet touches the depth of history are priceless. Speaking the truth, whether listened to or not, is the lesson. And the teaching.

"Fare forward, voyagers." T. S. Eliot's famous poetic rendering of Krishna's admonition to Arjuna on the field of battle. The world is the prophet's field of battle. That field of battle is endless.

"Fare forward" is a summation of the outer and inner contradictions of prophetic life. It provides a frame to ponder the mystery of the prophets and their persistence through history.

Keep on keeping on is activism, the important side of what needs to be done. Yet activism without depth is doomed. Activism without depth rings the bell of mutual despair.

We cannot afford despair. The prophetic knows this. The prophet lives this. Is this where the prophet and the prophetic part company? The doomed prophet. The prophetic community that surrounds the doomed prophet.

3

Negotiating the Prophetic

When we speak for others, we speak for ourselves. Our voice is entangled. Even the primal prophetic is negotiated. Our voice isn't only for others or ourselves. Our voice is an intermediary, a way of bridging the gap between I and the world.

I and the world. I and Thou, Martin Buber's sense of things. At the base of reality there is a foundational, mystical connection. I-Thou is balanced by I-It; we live in the material world. Not every moment of life can be Thou. We objectify our life to survive. The prophetic is about Thou and It, separated and intertwined. The political and economic systems of every time and place have to be scrutinized. Judgment is essential. The political and economic systems of society are called to task precisely when they crush the weak. In the Bible, the widow, the orphan, the poor and the stranger are victims of unjust systems. Their very being, their Thou, is under assault by a system that remakes persons into objects, It. To justify such an unjust system, God is objectified as well. People as objects. God as object.

Negotiating the Prophetic

When God becomes objectified all bets are off, or on, depending on where you stand in the "object" lineup. If you are riding the crest of the power wave, cathedrals are built for you to worship in. Those on the bottom sweep the floors. A counter-claim is made. Sweepers of the cathedrals will inherit the earth. The last will be first. God's Realm is for them.

Does God have a preferential love for the disinherited? Even those who believe God's reign will occur on earth, one day, must wonder. God's power on behalf of the disinherited is the great hope. The way for those on the bottom and those committed to justice to express hope that, at the end of the day, justice, Thou, will prevail. The disinherited embody the hope of a world beyond suffering and a God who wants such a world.

Yet the evidence for such a hope warrants exploration. If the disinherited are the favored ones, indeed the hope of the world and perhaps proof positive that a good and just God exists, why do the disinherited grow in numbers? When some of the disinherited make it to the other side of the river, why is it that others take their place? As we know well, sometimes the newly disinherited are created by the formerly disinherited.

The language we use to describe oppression is important. There is a boundary between political and religious speech. The prophetic is full throttle and doesn't mince words. Though the prophetic's claim is ultimately religious, it speaks in a ethical vein that is deeply political. The words "Holocaust" and "genocide" are instructive here. When every context of suffering is so described it loses its political edge. What am I—what are we—to do with these situations whose first appeal is overwhelming catastrophe? Is such terminology itself an appeal or argument with a God who is silent in the face of unjust suffering? The prophet sounds the alarm. Still, the undoing of suffering is a political rather than a religious task.

If the appeal to God is worthwhile, if tangible results are in the offing, then offering up religious terminology is like a prayer answered. Since, in the main, our prayers are rarely answered or we devise a system whereby whatever happens is a response, the appropriate course is to proceed in the political realm. Then, again, the political realm, is most often like unanswered prayers. Shall we keep offering up our hope to political systems whose interests rarely coincide with justice?

We are left in a quandary. Neither God nor our political systems are the answer. At times, both seemed viable. Or was this a historical confluence that is ascribed to God or politics—after? The belated ascription functions in the theoretical scheme of history, however, we would do well to avoid such schemes in the present. Calling on God or politics has its limited place. Reliance on either, though, is a sign of weakness. Both are messianic only in the rhetorical sense. Salvation, if such a concept is viable, and justice, if we parse it with grave limitations, lie Somewhere Else, quite near the voices we carry individually and collectively.

Left with our individual and, sometimes, collective voice, we feel weak. What is, overwhelms what we hope to be. Thus our outrage. What should be isn't and won't be, at least in our lifetime. For example, the pace of technological change is far quicker and more decisive than change in the economic and political structures of our world. As well, changes in technology help disguise or seemingly ameliorate the divisions in the world that, in real time, grow wider. The very resources needed for technological innovation, including cheap and dangerous labor, are built into the very advances we celebrate. Our notions of progress beg critical analysis. Paradoxically, that very analysis will be facilitated by the same technological innovation that oppresses. Which begs further questions as to whether the very people who seek to heal the divisions in our world unintentionally widen them.

With the battle lines drawn it is difficult to think in nuanced ways, even if nuance is where the truth, as far as we can apprehend it, might lie. Unfortunately, the fog of war reeks havoc on the military and the activist alike. Similarly, religion suffers when mobilized. Whether for empire or the prophetic, mobilized thought and spirituality loses its cutting edge. Here the suspicions surrounding committed thought are important: that the thinker activist who refuses to join the struggle on terms that mitigate independent thought might indeed be a double agent. In the face of suffering,

Negotiating the Prophetic

it is hard to take an independent position, lest it seem that the thoughtful activist is trimming her sails. Is the one who follows the beat of his own justice drummer distancing himself from the field of battle?

In seemingly intractable scenarios, it might be best to begin again with an "everything is lost" sensibility. The non-negotiable positions adopted by both sides rarely go anywhere. Even if the powers that be think they can hold on to their positions forever and the opposition knows they cannot, the suffering of the people in between is relentless. The position that change is inevitable is fine. However, knowing that the inevitable change will be in favor of those now presently suffering is often a matter of faith rather than politics.

Change is inevitable, the direction of change isn't. Arguing for the entire justice cake because it is the only honest thing to do is morally righteous. In life, though, since every personal and collective victory and defeat is negotiated, solutions to injustice are never complete. Paying up for past injuries, for example, is always partial.

The future, too, even if justice is pursued by all sides, will only be partially just. New causalities arise everywhere even in the best case scenario. The pursuit of justice, like life itself, is complicated and self-involved. As with healing and inclusion, the pursuit of justice involves injury, exclusion and death. Often the pursuit of justice is stillborn.

If everything in life is negotiated, so, too, the prophetic. Initially this seems counter-intuitive. As we perceive it, the prophet's hallmark is the opposite. If anyone in the world refuses to compromise with injustice it is the prophets. Though there is a truth in this appraisal, the notion that the prophet refuses to negotiate justice is misplaced.

This is true even with the biblical prophets. At the origin of their call the prophets are already negotiating with God. Are they righteous enough to be prophets? They are sure there is someone better suited. Throughout, the biblical prophets mediate God's will and Israel's backsliding, sometimes discouraging God from overreach, other times lamenting that God is too patient with Israel. On the punishment of Israel the prophets are likewise torn. With regard to Israel's sins, often God is scorched earth, yet the prophets, having announced punishment, are forced to witness Israel's suffering in real time. An unannounced theme of the prophets is that there must be another way.

The prophetic way isn't only about justice, especially a justice that overrides the possibility of ordinary life. For if the possibility of ordinary life is sacrificed for full justice, new victims will be created and, this, without the assurance that justice for victims will be achieved. The issue here is less perfection than the concrete movement toward justice. If speed and totality are the only means possible, sooner than later the prophets will be confronted with a new injustice. More victims will be created by the rulers who, while allowing little compromise with the former victors, are themselves corrupted by the spoils of victory.

The primal prophetic voice is caught between untold suffering and the alleviation of that suffering as a way to improve the lot of the victims, all the while creating new victims or at least the potential that accompanies revolutionary fervor. For these reasons the prophet is unable to stand on the sidelines or completely identify with the resistance to oppression.

Remaining on the sidelines to some extent, even amid the struggle, is the price to be paid for a vigilance that refuses a superficial loyalty to the oppressed. Identification with the oppressed is crucial but the question of when that identification becomes another form of blindness is paramount. How can the primal prophetic voice identify with the victims without courting the possibility that, if the tables are turned, a voice that sounds the next alarm will be needed? The next alarm must be anticipated even before the tables are turned and since, at least in our time, table turning is less likely, the primal prophetic voice is in a more difficult situation.

Crying out for justice too long is perilous. Our energy is limited and the temptation toward cynicism is great. Other voices are raised. Most of them come and go, some are bought off, others

Negotiating the Prophetic

lose interest quickly and disappear. The prophetic sensibility has to be aware of the long haul and that the possibility of success is remote. And today, without being able to claim God as the prophet's author, sustenance is an abiding issue. Where are the resources for the prophetic long haul? Where do they come from and what allows some on the prophetic path to continue while others fade away?

The perils of the prophetic are many. They include: ego, cynicism, becoming a cult figure, being rejected by the conservative and progressive elite, being accepted by them. More: wanting to be accepted, wanting to be rejected, making money from your prophetic vision, being impoverished by it. Still more: feeling that if only the world accepts your way the world will be different, feeling that your voice and the voices of others do not matter. Finally: looking back and seeing your prophetic vision as a failure, thinking that those who go beyond your vision are going too far, not caring about depth, wanting too much depth.

The Long Haul Prophetic is itself a negotiation. The prophet has been around and seen it all. There are phases of the prophetic life and the primal prophetic voice changes over time. The mark of the long haul prophet is constancy within change, an evolution within a single angle of vision; remaining until the end, even after, without marking time and without craving the spotlight. In some ways the prophetic is like performing on a revolving stage. When your time is up you arrive at a different place within the same theater.

This hardly means the primal prophetic voice is above the fray, lacks envy, doesn't want it all and then some. The prophet is not above human nature, the ordinary run of things, desire, making mistakes, being turned away, turning away others. The prophetic voice you hear has been heard before but turns in an exceptional way, within a tradition, which means the prophet's claim to either stand in the tradition only or to be completely unique are both dead-ends. Nonetheless, the prophetic voice before you is always a one-off. Despite all we know and have experienced about the prophets, each prophetic voice is a mysterious encounter with the deepest part of our humanity. We want to turn away. We can't.

PROPHET-SHARING

Derided, lauded, dismissed, elevated, worried about, envied or despised, we turn away from the one who arrives at our peril. For even those who know the score, all of a sudden something is spoken, which we somehow know but haven't been able to put together quite like this and, besides, there is an edge in his voice, a cadence, a depth that is elusive, hardly quantifiable, yet remains long after the words are spoken. The prophet's voice remains in the moment, her words spoken at a depth and urgency that shakes us to our core.

The prophet's words carry a people's history, judging it with a hope and compassion that compels us. We cannot turn away from the prophetic one, nor can we turn away from the depth that forces a reckoning with our community's history and ourselves. The prophetic voice places us right at our center, which we would like to turn away from, too, and cannot. Until the moment arrives when we no longer want to turn away. We embrace the moment before us. Such is the prophetic voice, so singular and, against the grain, now shared.

Can the prophetic voice be shared so the prophet's voice becomes ours? Is the prophetic within all of us, as some kind of primal inheritance, that for reasons unknown is more articulate in some than in others? The prophet is not only a one-off, she is rarely found at all. When and where the next prophet will popup is anyone's guess. We lack prophet predictors, a calculus that can be consulted, as if the prophets are on a timetable. And though Jews have first call on the prophetic, the prophetic being the Jewish indigenous, the prophetic tradition has spread far and wide.

Prophet-sharing is the coin of the realm these days and the prophetic back-and-forth between communities is a positive addition, indeed expansion, of the prophetic tradition. This means cross pollination in the geographic, cultural, and religious realms

Negotiating the Prophetic

and a solidarity that re-presents the prophetic to communities losing their prophetic edge. Prophet-sharing is the new interfaith ecumenical dialogue starting point or, better, the path to a new solidarity across religious lines. To a large extent this is already happening and though the diminishment of, say, mainstream Protestant denominations, is explained in various ways, their diminishment may have something to do with prophet-sharing. Without having a name, the shared prophetic has rendered Christian denominational life less and less relevant.

Does the shared prophetic mean shared hope? Shared suffering? A shared political and religious vision? The shared prophetic is a mutual challenge. The shared prophetic is a mutual alarm system. When one community's prophetic is asleep at the wheel, another community's prophetic can shake the slumbering community awake. Many questions remain, of course. The shared prophetic signals the emergence of a new community, with its own particularity and traditions that cross over the old, increasingly irrelevant, communal divisions. What, then, happens to the old divisions that, though no longer whole or life giving, remain as shattered resource fragments for a new beginning?

Taking the good of the old traditions and leaving the bad behind has much to recommend it. Rarely is that which lasts only bad or void of possibility, especially when turned around and looked at in a new light. Still, the division between communities which arose in the tumult of history has deep roots and continues to yield distinctives that shape the human journey. The most obvious division between Jews and Christians, for example, is Jesus as the Christ. No matter how Jesus is parsed among progressive Christians, Jesus is likely to continue to divide. Now add historical figures within the Christian tradition, for example, Martin Luther. For those who identify with Luther, no matter their apologies for his dark anti-Semitic side, it is difficult to see how Jews can embrace even the shattered fragments of Luther's theological insights. Other divisions are likewise fraught, in America for example, between the white and Black communities, each with their own histories and traditions. Despite the shared vision of many whites and Blacks, their life experience continues to diverge in important ways. Is the prophet-sharing of Martin Luther King Jr., between whites and Blacks, a flesh-and-blood sharing or an illusion?

The end of the old divisions—possible? The cleansing of traditions that pretend to be whole—in process? The reinterpretation of the traditions is ongoing. Yet we know that these processes, while clearly progressive, hide sins being committed today. Progressive liturgies, as inclusive and pleasing to the ear as they are, need critical, prophetic analysis. The interruption necessary is bound to upset many. After all, isn't purification and renewal what the prophets plead for? The Vatican II conclave and its liturgical reforms, so revolutionary, is confronted by Latin American liberation theology, and comes up short. Women in the rabbinate, so revolutionary, is confronted by Israel's oppression of the Palestinian people, and comes up short. Just when communities take a step forward, it seems they take one or two steps backward.

A confessional prophetic solidarity? A beginning for sure and difficult enough. Still a deeper reckoning has to take place. The very religious symbols employed, the Cross first among them, though now joined by the Star of David, because of their blessing of injustice, indict the very center of religious particularities. Without losing track of the essential, most powerful, religious symbol of modernity, progress. Symbols that stand at the center of even confessional fragments of the imperialist whole remain problematic. Arguing that everything wayward in history was an aberration, and thus the central religious symbols can be cleansed and retrieved, is problematic. Once modernity rejects its core, progress, it likewise enters a similar situation. These compromised symbols, say the Cross and modernity, are centers of meaning for their adherents. Where do the followers of Christianity and modernity go if their altars are removed?

Altars, like Gods, are always appearing. In human history there has rarely been an altar/God void. Stand-ins for the true God are just waiting for their time on center stage. But, then, how do we know that the One True God isn't a stand-in? Matriarchal Gods as well. Perhaps this is why ancient Israel's God is without a name.

Being nameless, though, didn't keep the biblical writers from filling in the blanks.

Are prophets stand-ins for the unnamed God? In being sent by God and carrying God's message, the prophets secured their mission and protection. Yet their missions were mostly failures, their protection less than stellar. Think of Jesus and Paul as latecomers to the mission-protection parade. The Hebrew prophets fared little better. So, returning to confession, it seems that once we come to the end of our particular altar/God inheritance line we are thrown into another altar/God ring. Our secular believers are in the same ring really. They are just more naive about their "No Altar/God Found Here" signs above their Temple of Progress worship sites than those critically-thinking religious folks who come to the end of their line, wondering where to go.

Perhaps there is nowhere to go, and this "nowhere" is precisely where it all began. When the prophets appeared, Israel wasn't going anywhere except empire and oppression. Wherever the prophets gained their insight and fortitude, however, they described their supernatural partner as otherworldly and as an intimate. We have the biblical writers and their editors, redactors and interpreters, a veritable scribal and clerical industry to thank for this naming.

Now the prophets are safely and unsafely in the hands of the academic-seminary industrial complex. These latest redactors seem to know everything about the prophets and their God, perhaps even more than the prophets and God knew. What heady knowledge! Some biblical scholars know so much about the prophets and God, they preside over a divine-like transmission that infuses the modern classroom with a Sinai-like drama.

We have sparse knowledge of the origins of the prophets or the God or spirit that commanded them and sent them on their perilous way. How the prophets come down to us is likely skewed, perhaps even unintelligible to those who were present at the creation. The importance of the prophets resides elsewhere than divining their origins.

Whether their God or not, the textual God of the prophets is now our God. With the proviso that "our God" needs to be interrupted, indeed has been interrupted already by history and the fact, rather than theological ruminations, that God is rarely, if ever, a rescuer or a liberator. It is less than obvious that God is saving us, the world or creation, no matter how insistent, beautiful and inclusive our prayers are.

Modernity isn't saving us either, progress on all fronts being as much illusion as real. Still, why give up for the God that does not save, or rescue, or grant us an earthly sanctuary where all will live as equals in peace? Yes, each to her own God in the private sphere; morning devotions and Sabbath gatherings have their place. To mistake these private devotions for a public religiosity, however, is problematic. For the most part, the biblical prophets were low on prayer and liturgy. They spent more time on the road, speaking their truth to power, challenging those who pedaled empire religion, and speaking directly to God. A God who sometimes heard, other times ignored and, only once in a while, directly responded.

PROPHETIC HOPE—WITHIN DISASTER

With some exceptional moments, God sends the prophets on their way and lets them fend for themselves. The prophets have to think on their feet and, when necessary, think while running for their life. No one reading the biblical prophets should think of the prophet's journey as one protected by God. It seems that, though the God of Israel has justice on his mind and needs messengers, God lets thing play out as they will. The concept of free will, European Enlightenment style, is hardly the biblical way. American pragmatism rarely appears in the Bible either. Once accepting God's summons, the prophets are bound.

The all-encompassing covenantal web constricts the choices of Israel and the prophets themselves. Still, the prophets are constantly making decisions within God's command and sometimes on their own. The fate of the prophets is failure large and small, even if in certain confrontations with power the prophets come out on top.

One fears collapse in the biblical text. The prophets' victories are shadowed by failure, their narrow escapes are hardly assured. We sit on the edge of our biblical seats as the prophets duck out of harm's way or flee for their lives. We sense that down the line the prophets will misstep or even fall in a pre-ordained defeat. Still, even as the empire's visionaries argue their case, the prophets stubbornly refuse to assimilate to unjust power. The disaster in the cards as we read the Bible is contemporary as well. Then and now, the prophets are doomed. Prophet-sharing is thus disaster-sharing. Do the prophets within disaster also share hope?

The hope of the biblical prophets is Israel restored—to God—through justice. When justice fails to be established, exile it is. Israel's assimilation to unjust power puts Israel over the top. The die having been cast, God has had enough. First, though, through verbal and physical warnings, the prophets are placed or place themselves in danger. This hardly means that the prophets are free of fear, far from it. Often with reservation, sometimes with hesitation, the prophets walk with their fear. Though life threatening dangers are close at hand, the crux of the matter is less the present than Israel's legacy and the fate of the world that God has proclaimed on behalf of a people of little note.

The prophets who stand up to injustice today are in the same position as the biblical prophets, significantly, though, without the ability to proclaim God. Instead, for the first time in history the prophets are crossing communal boundaries in great numbers, and when the battle becomes intense, they provide each other shelter. In the Bible, Isaiah refers to his need for shelter from the storm. Needed then. Needed now.

Our storm isn't only now and it isn't only coming from the failed promise of modern life. The storm is humanity crashing at the gates of ecological sustainability and political equality, producing so much more, and flourishing so much less. Our Wheel of Wellbeing is on the verge of being thrown into overdrive. The prophet laments that what is loss cannot be regained. As well, the prophet points to the hope of beginning again. Yet the prophet knows that the beginning-again time has passed. With all of us, the prophet is caught in the crosshairs.

Like those in exile, the prophetic today is caught in the crosshairs without God, at least a God who commands and directs history. Whatever direction we take, we travel on our own terms. Whether our direction is locatable on a typical theological map is doubtful. Bereft of an external ordering, we search for order within. That order is threatened by the trauma we experience, or the trauma we know will come. The knock on the door comes when we least expect it. Having experienced the knock or experienced it through others, life is never the same. Hope takes on a different hue, if hope survives. Tomorrow is less a new beginning than another possibility of interrupted life.

After trauma, whatever comes our way is processed in a more somber light. Justice around the corner is for the neophyte. With justice delayed, hope turns elsewhere. For prophetic hope is otherworldly, within the world. Prophetic hope is, on occasion, imagining another way of life, participating in and thinking through it, praying, and singing the songs that take us away from the harsh reality that limits healing. The trauma we experience, or is right around the corner, is a collective trauma, too. The prophet rarely passes her time as if a better life beyond this world exists. It doesn't.

Knowing that justice is rare and momentary and that the aim has to be evolutionary, more justice over time, incrementally, while those who shout the loudest want justice whole and now, the prophet maintains her vigilance. Without giving in to apathy or a hope that simply satisfies our own voice, this road is a difficult one to travel. It is hard traveling light when suffering increases daily, yet being weighed down by trauma and hopelessness won't do either. The children are the way forward. Their turn on the stage is a form of hope. Knowing what we know, though, how do we counsel them forward? Trauma lies ahead for our children, too.

Is there no comfort for the afflicted and the prophets that travel with them? The prophets who come from the affluent and those who come from the other side of the tracks—another form

Negotiating the Prophetic

of prophet-sharing—learn from each other. The interfaith dialogue has no place to hide here. Divisions in justice issues hardly matter, even if at first you want to clarify why you are in the prophetic mix, here and not there. As in: "I'm here with you because I am a _____." Fill in the blank if you care to, but Jew, Christian, Muslim or secular means little in the trenches. Or, it might mean a lot in the heat of battle. Whatever strengthens one's resolve is likely to change as the prophetic community moves forward together.

Shared commitment and suffering, small victories and defeat, the absurdity of much of life, inverted politics and endless war, all that bring tears and laughter to our lives renders irrelevant the various doxologies we initially bring to our solidarity table. Which, paradoxically, is where we are most alone, especially after the battle has been fought, with more battles on the horizon.

For in any solidarity worth its salt, we find a solitude that deepens with each passing year. The biblical prophets are engaged—and alone. So, too, and perhaps even more so, those in the prophetic line today are engaged—and alone. If, beyond pious organizing platitudes, we enter deeply into solidarity.

The danger is that activists and their activities may become cheerleaders that wrestle to the ground those who dare to think in "incorrect" terms. Like, understanding that empire has many sides, some of which are intriguing and beneficial. Like, understanding that democracy and equality are two important but limited sensibilities. Like, understanding that one person's universalism can be another person's oppression. Like, understanding that communities are distinctive and that individual sensibilities are often found within a broader collective. Like, understanding that there are prophets, one-offs, whose primary task is to probe history, philosophy and theology at the deepest level rather than being welcomed as a team player.

There is a time for togetherness and for being alone. What a shame it would be if we lost the interplay of solitude and solidarity, the central tension of life. Those in exile who experience trauma as a way of life know this tension well. It is like the believer who experiences God and then God's absence, then God's return, with absence following. Thereafter, life takes on a pattern that has little rhyme or reason, without a timetable for presence and absence. If the believer is honest, absence predominates; solidarity is often an unrequited hope. For even in solidarity, betrayal is frequent, as self-interest and grandstanding are the names of the game. Even small victories are sullied. During the prophetic journey we are thrown back on ourselves through thick and thin.

THE PERSISTENCE OF THE PROPHETIC

The prophets in retreat. In the Bible, prophets retreat frequently. In our mind, though, the prophets are at the barricades. True enough, but not only. Even the engaged prophet, thundering commitment, return and destiny, is often alone. For the prophets, retreat is a tactic, often a need.

When the biblical prophets speak the truth as it was given to them by God, the prophet is deeply rooted. Rootedness overcomes fear. When the hunt for the prophet is on, though, the prophet's anxiety runs high. The prophet hopes God will provide shelter. It matters little if the shelter provided is through divine intervention or human surrogates. The shelter provided prophets by humans is divided, sometimes prompted by God's intervention and, other times, by human freelancing.

Either way, shelter is temporary. Fleeing or in hiding, the prophet is vulnerable. The danger is dual, to the prophet's person and to the prophet's mission. I doubt that the prophet remains as sure of her mission as the Bible sometimes relates, even so, the prophet's anxiety surfaces in the text and remains whether God is present or absent. Both are dealt with by the prophet with a freelance energy that might come from God's original command—should we call this Divine Surplus?—or from the prophet's determination to carry on almost as a form of defiance. Should we call these moments above and beyond divine and human capabilities, Prophetic Surplus?

Prophetic Surplus, as if the prophet's life and soul depended on keeping on. The poet, Adrienne Rich, wrote that "often such

Negotiating the Prophetic

truths come by accident, or from strangers." It is a leap of faith that the prophet's ability to remain faithful to the end has to do only with God or only with truth. The truth that often comes by accident, or from strangers often plays a role and, though they largely remain anonymous or are known by name only in their interaction with the prophet's journey, their freelancing is essential. The truth remains; the prophets cannot rely only on God or their comrades-in-arms. The prophet's ability to pull herself up and off the mat and stand on her own two feet when the going is toughest is the human drama writ large.

The prophet is one step ahead—or behind—the collapse of meaning. Is he also one step ahead—or behind—the collapse of God? In the Bible the collapse of God is hinted at. Jesus' quite Jewish last words of being forsaken are clear. Christianity cleans up this collapse as religions do, as the Abandoned One becomes the vehicle for salvation. Rabbinic Judaism buries its head in biblical texts that, in the hands of the rabbis, become allegorical. The modern prophets and prophetic community are denied this deflection. Would it then be better to abandon the notion of God altogether? After all, prophets of all stripes are perpetually on the run. That trauma is enough. Do we need the additional trauma, perhaps the trauma of traumas, by dwelling on the God question when everyone knows the answer is, at best, elusive?

The question of God can be argued. It can be buried, as it is often in Christianity and Islam. Secular prophetic voices dismiss God as an ancient trope, left to the weak and right-wing bigots. Yet their God, the God of Modernity, is now on the docket. Humanity barely survived the traditional God of Israel and its Christian variant. Humanity might not survive the insatiable God of Modernity. So, on the one hand, best to scrap the entire God enterprise? On the other hand, there will always be a God that is worshipped, named as such, or not. Then there is the real question of the prophet's life. Why suffer for others, why insist there is a destiny to be fulfilled, why persevere when our journey might be without meaning?

At first glance, the question of meaning seems out of place. Destiny as well. What does God have to do with either? Slamming the door on these questions is fine, as long as we realize they will continue to exist in history, in our lives and in the lives of our communities. The meaning/destiny/God questions remain.

Our insistence, especially when we negate all of these questions, is telling. In life, final solutions elude us, only ongoing negotiations, conducted in a myriad of ways, remain. There are few better ways to testify to important questions than by answering them with force. Like Jews who are obsessed with the question of Israel and justice for Palestinians who insist that it is only injustice, rather than Jewishness and Jewish history, that prompts their commitment. Or the criticism of Cornel West on his too-heavy critique of Barack Obama during Obama's presidency, as if West's critique of Obama wasn't heavily influenced by their shared Blackness and West's feeling that somehow Obama had betrayed Black history.

The same goes for Edward Said, the late Palestinian intellectual, who knew it all for years, but then became unhinged when Yasser Arafat sold out the Palestinian people—Palestinian history?—by signing the Oslo Accords in 1993. As if Jews, Blacks, and Palestinians are universalists. Even the so-called universal is caught up in the particular, and the particular is nothing if not about meaning/destiny/God. Rather than answering these questions, though, the particular, even when it masquerades as the universal, is involved in highlighting and negotiating them.

The prophets know this well. The prophets stand at the crossroads where these questions lead. For when the arena is meaning/destiny/God, communal and individual responses are fraught. The prophet cries out that everything is at stake, more or less, all the time. Which makes the prophet impossible to bear—for all sides.

Negotiating with meaning/destiny/God, whether we slam the door shut, open it wide or just crack the door and peer inside, there is no way out. As unfinished beings, our ends haunt us. And the prophet once again ups the ante. Throwing herself against the tide of history, then being thrown against the tide, the prophet has no choice but to embody the negotiation of ultimates. As if she carries the weight of these questions for others. Or with others.

Negotiating the Prophetic

Regardless, what is at stake in humanity's journey is highlighted by and, as importantly, within the prophet.

Prophetic movements, whether consciously or not, embody this negotiation, too. Therefore every victory, and more often every defeat, involves more than meets the eye. For the prophet, everything is at stake all the time; there is no rest for the weary prophet. The exile that the prophet and, later, the prophetic community experiences, is the place of testing. The longer in exile the higher the stakes. So prophet-sharing is a high stakes affair. For if one community fails the test, other communities can pick up the slack. If the prophet-sharing community fails as a whole no one is left to pick up the pieces.

The collapse of God in our time falls most heavily on the prophet. For the prophet is the one who is supposed to know the score and, very importantly, articulate the score to the powerful as a confrontation and to the oppressed who are looking for a way out of an apparently hopeless situation. Yet the prophet is conflicted. Speaking truth to power, the prophet has to speak truth to herself. That truth is up in the air. It is easier to speak of what ails society than to determine the intricacies of solutions. The political, economic, and ecological pie the prophet seeks to re-divide is too interconnected, stubborn, full of material complexities and human frailty.

The prophet knows that the justice people need right now is seen as injustice by those who have what they need. Moreover, the idea that the oppressed are—only—innocent in their powerlessness, or would be if they achieved power, is naive. The prophet cannot afford such a romanticized view of the world. And the notion that God is among the oppressed and will empower the oppressed, well, the prophet has only to look around to see how rarely justice works out that way. In our time, biblical God-talk, though still employed, is, in efficacious terms, far behind us. Even those who speak of the God of the Oppressed know that God is rarely a leader or a rescuer.

Through this collapse, human and divine, with the flaws that spread from sea to shining sea and beyond, how do we account for the persistence of the prophetic? For those who believe in miracles that alter nature and the logic of human endeavor, the persistence of the prophetic is of a different order. For those who know that miracles are mostly agents of deception and superstition, the persistence of the prophetic is the challenge of challenges. For if through thick and thin, with and without God, the prophets keep arriving, our human and divine compass needs readjusting.

The persistence of the prophets alters our routine assumptions, rote allegiances, insistent hope, and constant despair. The persistence of the prophetic hardly proves or disproves any concept, creed, or ideology. Rather, the persistence of the prophets/prophetic is a pure and simple marvel that disabuses us of the categories we construct to stabilize our social, political and religious life. When the prophet arrives, all is unsettled. Trouble, once on the horizon, is back in town.

ISRAEL'S UNSTABLE GOD

The prophets are constant trouble. Instability is the prophet's wake. Is this because the God that originally called the prophets is unstable? At least by the definitions of God we prefer, the guarantor of life, making sense of the unintended, the tragic, children dying before their time, the biblical God of Israel is a God we rely on at our peril.

Reasoning with God, a platform that Moses performed admirably at times, is possible. Confronting God, again like Moses did when Israel was about to become the battering ram of God's anger, is possible. The most telling point is that God's biblically chosen, Israel, is itself unstable. Or rather the prophets and God's hallmark is an instability that was, paradoxically, Israel's stability.

Taking it a step further, the relationship between God and Israel features instability as its stability. We know this because whenever God or Israel attempted to pursue a normal path, it was upended by one or both. It seems that upending stability kept both God and Israel on their toes, challenging and admonishing each other, but also remaining in relationship. They may have feared

Negotiating the Prophetic

that if either left the relationship both would be more than alone. God and Israel would be adrift in the universe, without purpose, their intertwined destiny unwound.

Today the unstable stability of ancient Israel is a distant memory. When remembered at all, it is dissected by academics or reenacted liturgically by rabbis and ministers. Yet the root of the prophetic continues among the heirs of ancient Israel, Jews, and the sought after stability by Jews around the world, especially in the state of Israel, has obviously failed. Even in the wake of the Holocaust, the Jewish prophetic has reawakened, making the Jewish search for stability in a post-Holocaust Jewish state seem like a head-long flight to assimilate to unjust power.

The struggle against that assimilation is the raison d'être of the contemporary Jewish prophetic, mostly without mention of and often allied against any conception of God. Ostensibly universalist, it is the most particular intervention of a small, yet, globally dispersed community that harkens back to the Diaspora riches of commitment to justice around the world. In this, the contemporary Jewish prophetic shares its resources with other communities and allies with them.

Yet here, once again, notions of the universal sit uneasily. For the Jewish prophetic is a specifically Jewish project even when it is applied to the world outside the Jewish community. After all, it is the refusal of Jewish assimilation that is first and foremost. While "Jewish" seems too small for Jewish universalists, it is telling that the universal is applied so vigorously on their Jewish stage.

Performing the Jewish prophetic, in Israel and elsewhere, is most true at home where the biblical prophetic originated. Is this why the contemporary Jewish prophetic is so fierce, uncompromising and destabilizing? This, after what was supposed to be the final homecoming of Israel. By home, though, I don't mean only the state of Israel. By home I mean within the dynamic of Jewish life, the endless civil wars which define Jewish history, the very continuation of which we see once again in our time.

Surprise, surprise, the Jewish prophetic has returned home at the time when the Jewish civil wars were supposed to be over, when, after the Holocaust, the prophetic was thought dead and buried. To start another Jewish civil war when everything is finally settled and Jews, after almost being annihilated in the Holocaust, have finally emerged empowered, is incredible. Is it?

Thankfully for advocates of Jewish power, God, too, had already been buried. Where was God in Auschwitz? The Holocaust mantra is that Jews are alone, God and humanity being AWOL, and thus have to empower themselves. Then unexpectedly, out of the blue, the Jewish prophetic reemerges, slowly but surely, first drawing an ethical border around Jewish empowerment, then challenging Jewish empowerment itself, as if Jews can and must reenter the world in solidarity with others. As a command? Imagine—a post-Holocaust world without a Jewish state at all! The Jewish prophetic voice is increasingly found here, risking a final instability rather than sanctioning the permanent oppression of another people. Raising the question: Have the Jewish prophets gone insane?

The definition of insanity being? It is difficult to think that the use of Jewish power to permanently oppress the Palestinian people is sane. As if sanity demands violating almost every ethical norm known to Jewish history, then to go one step further, then another. When one thinks the state of Israel, with the enabling of the American Jewish establishment, has reached the bottom and ethical depravity has nowhere to descend, it reaches another level. Jewish ethical violations seems to be without a bottom, as other empire powers know well. Yet, though there is always dissent within empire. The Jewish prophets know what the possible charges are. And what the possible outcome of dissent may be.

Since Jews know what the powers of this world can do to a defenseless people. Then to do to another defenseless people what in some ways was done to Jews, what shame, the destruction of an entire history, Jewish to begin with, so that Jews can become like the Other Nations the Bible calls out? Did the Jewish establishment in Israel and America think that empowerment could discipline and bury the prophetic forever? In a sense they did, thus the development of Holocaust theology which placed the Holocaust—and

Negotiating the Prophetic

Israel—off-limits to rational discussion and critique. As if the proposed lesson that what the Holocaust teaches—more and more power, more and more armaments, more and more oppression—would be accepted without a fight.

In a world of the powerful and the weak, after so much suffering, shouldn't Jews do anything to come out on top? Only fleetingly considered was the other path, that Jews need empowerment as do all peoples, thus the hope to build an interdependent empowerment. This would be somewhat like prophet-sharing, where each person and community looks out for the other and, when one veers off course or is assaulted, others stand ready to fill the breach.

The very definition of sanity and practical ways forward is up for grabs, since every form of power, unilateral or shared, has to be negotiated, why not refuse the solitude of unilateral empire and instead move toward an interdependent solidarity? Though an interdependent solidarity will always be imperfect, it nonetheless lays the groundwork for the possibility that never again will Jews or any people be so alone as the Jews of Europe were and now Palestinians are.

With more and more power, the ethical collapse is obvious. Soon the collapse of the Jewish state? The great "another Holocaust" fear is deeply ingrained in Jews. Despite having power, unexpectedly, Jewish fear increases. With Jewish backs against the ethical wall will the necessary reckoning become more and more difficult? Impossible? The prophets are there to pick up the pieces. Where do they start? When do they finish? When they finish, what will be left of Jewish life?

The stakes are high. Millions of Jewish and Palestinian lives are on the line. So the prophets have no choice but to speak. Out loud. For all the world to hear the sins of Israel, once again the Jewish prophetic returns to its origins. Strange how many Jews of Conscience think they are a *novum* in Jewish history or are just saying what they would be saying anywhere for anyone. But everyone knows that the stakes, at least for Jews, are highest here. That is why the Jewish prophetic voice heard around the world on almost every issue has, itself, been retreating, coming back to the Jewish home they thought they left behind. Jews left their Jewish home because it was too restrictive and filled with the hypocrisy—idolatry?

DISSIDENT ISRAELIS

Jews of Conscience are being driven over the edge by the seventy plus years occupation of Palestinians and Israel's wars against Palestinians that come with increasing regularity. So the broken pieces of ethical Jewish life continue to break into more and more pieces until the possibility of solving the Jewish puzzle wanes. Jews, having returned to Israel, continue to dissent and often leave Israel and their Jewishness behind, because they, rather than God, see no repentance, no justice and no hope. And shame of all shames, according at least to the Jewish establishment in Israel and America, some of these Jewish Israeli leave-takers will return to Israel only when it is replaced by Palestine. Some Jews of Conscience in Israel and beyond do not pine for the Jewish state, they pine for Palestine!

If a Jew distances herself from being Israeli and Jewish does she become less or more Israeli and Jewish? Apply the same question to Christians and Muslims. Many Christians and Muslims want to be far away from what both their religions have been historically. As is often the case in life, less is more. Our identity formations aren't going anywhere. It is what we do with them that counts. But, again, on the Jewish side of things, deconstructing Jewishness has been the thing to do since the beginning of Jewish history.

Deconstructing Jewishness is the essence of the prophetic. Also constructing Jewishness. The prophets are deconstructors and constructors, tearing down the normative, rebuilding what was or what was supposed to be, that never ending—ever existing?—Jewish Golden Age. The Jewish Golden Age, when the hunt for freedom and justice was the call coming from and working with the Exodus God, Israel's God of Liberation.

That liberating God is the God Jews can still recall. Israel's God—*that was*. The covenant—*that was*. Is God and the covenant, now distant, remembered only through the embodiment by the

Negotiating the Prophetic

prophets? Because the prophets can no longer claim God hardly means that the headlong flight from Israel's injustice and the Jewish community's assimilation to unjust power is without the memory of God and the covenant. Such a memory might even be the unannounced and unconscious fuel that powers Jews inside and outside of Israel to protest the misdirection of Jewish history.

Alas, in their protest, Jews are staring their prophetic right in the face, calling the prophetic tradition as it exists today to account, as too tame, being read periodically in the synagogues, disciplined by the rabbis and thrown overboard by the Jewish community's embrace of injustice. The prophets ask whether this culpable Jewishness can hold its own while articulating and presenting itself to the world without engaging in wholesale deception.

Israelis are the Jewish boots on the ground. More and more leave Israel. Have they actually left? Dissident Israelis cross forbidden boundaries. Are they true boundary crossers? Like other dissenting Jews, they refuse to believe in God. For most, the very question of belief is archaic. Why bother? Their dismissal of God, though, is so strong as to become another attachment. Monotheism, even within the collapse of Jewish ethical life and the rage it engenders among the prophets, is a hard habit to break. Monotheism is addictive, and if you come from a community that has practiced and enforced this belief for thousands of years, you cannot give it up in a heartbeat or because a Jewish state has gone off the rails. Just the opposite, attention to idolatry infuses the monotheistic mindset with another battlefield, this time against those who claim God is on their side while practicing injustice.

When empire claims God what should one expect from the prophets except to refuse belief and the language of God altogether? Therefore it is unsurprising that dissident Israelis sometimes abandon Holocaust symbolism as well. To their mind, the Holocaust has become a surrogate God for Jews. So as the Jewish prophets attack Israel and deride the misuse of the Holocaust as surrogate God-language, they ignore traditional God-language and declare it irrelevant. While the debate about how the Holocaust functions and how far Israel will go in oppressing Palestinians rages on, most dissident Israelis think the God question is beyond the pale. For these Israelis, opening the debate about God in a situation of injustice smacks of idolatry.

So the Jewish prophetic is the boundary-crosser par excellence, except when it comes to God. Even the various love affairs some Jews have with other religions paradoxically hold this line. Those drawn to Buddhism, the Other Nations' religion of choice for spiritually inclined prophetic Jews of our time, steers clear of issues of divinity. Those drawn to Hinduism experience a cafeteria of Gods where choices can change and ultimate loyalty is left to choice. The few Jews drawn to Christianity provide a field day for psychologists, many of whom are Jews. For psychology is itself akin to a religion. There, loyalty is judged by the very distance one keeps from declaring a monotheistic God.

Leaving Israel, dissident Israelis appear in the Diaspora, Jewish or otherwise. You would think they had enough "Jewish" for a lifetime and, when asked, they respond that they have had enough in quite colorful language. Sometimes they use their native language, Hebrew. Other times, they respond in their newly adopted language. The tone and meaning are the same. Is their separation another commentary on the Jewish history they cannot leave? Since as Jews, former or not, they seem compelled to narrate their slice of Jewish history. Like the biblical slice they would rather not talk about, though their narration is so similar to the Bible, it is remarkable.

So dissident Israelis who flee Israel speak and write incessantly about it, again like their exiled biblical ancestors. There is a difference, though, since the exile of dissident Israelis is voluntary, characterized by rage and conscience, rather than forced by God. And the carnage they experienced in Israel was of another people, the carnage they caused. Some come to a point where they are unable to carry out the mission assigned to them by the state of Israel. Because their assignment is a post-Holocaust empowerment unfettered by Jewish ethics or international law? It is as if the biblical promise of land, once taken by force, is being abandoned by them, precisely because of the cost forced upon another people.

Negotiating the Prophetic

The Jewish community disciplines the prophetic, successfully for a time. The Holocaust and the threat of its return can do that for years, even decades. The Holocaust wasn't a hoax or a lark; theological reflections on the Holocaust appropriately pushed God to the margins. By doing so, however, there was an unintended result. God, on the ropes, returned, though this time dressed as an Israeli settler on Palestinian land, a right-wing zealot. The Jewish prophetic, also on the ropes, returned as well, fiery and unrepentant. Meanwhile, in the middle, Constantinian Jews plied the capitalist seas of white privilege as a colonial and imperial elite.

Brandishing a Holocaust sword and American imperial power, Constantian Jews set out to remake the world in their image. Israel is the centerpiece, at least symbolically, first as a place in the sun for the victims of the Holocaust, then as an exemplar of democracy in the unwashed sea of the Arab world. With Israel's increasing isolation in the world, now it is more or less power for power's sake, often mimicking the Republican Party's ideal vision of white American global power.

PROPHETIC ASCETICISM AND THE DESTITUTE OTHER

An asceticism, for the prophet, like the training of a fighter. When the battle is raging the prophet carries asceticism deep within. This doesn't mean the prophet is undisturbed when she is blindsided, tackled from behind and pummeled. At that moment, the prophet is like everyone else who has no escape.

The asceticism the prophet practices provides the resources for her to get up off the mat, right herself and continue on. Asceticism enables the prophet to negotiate the traumas of the exile life and reappear on the world's stage. Especially in colonized space, which is more or less everywhere if you think deeply about coloniality, negotiating trauma by way of asceticism is crucial.

When moments of celebration arrive, as they do sometimes, the prophet is ready to emerge from her dark interiors and bask in the light around her. The prophet is ready to embrace light wherever it comes from, often from the oppressed. The prophet without the asceticism of a fighter is impossible. But, then, the question remains as to where this light within and around the prophet leads to? Since it rarely leads to justice or the end of exile. Light, more light, the moment when the prophet is surrounded by light, can we imagine the embattled and traumatized prophet happy?

Yes, with reference to Israel's militarism, a symbolic inversion, some have visions of Star of David Helicopter Gunships in the Ark of the Covenant. To be substituted for the Torah scrolls? How dare the image cross the mind of Jews! It hardly takes an overactive imagination to see that such images take on a life of their own. Having been thought, though, militarized Judaism, a Jewishness that has taken up the sword, fighter aircraft, and the drone death machine, well, it was only a matter of time until the Jewish prophetic explored the imaginary terrain of the real. Star of David Helicopter Gunships in the Ark of the Covenant make the most perfect sense for the arrival and legitimating of Constantinian Judaism.

Being a Christian off-shoot, the Jewish establishment and Judaism itself in bed with the state, perhaps the synagogue should offer communion rails and incense on the High Holy Days. An Easter egg hunt before Passover on the nicely manicured synagogue grounds as well? A Christmas tree lighting ceremony in the synagogue lobby?

Just like prophet-sharing, Constantinian-sharing among the various empire contingents is the order of the day. It is easy to bury the hatchet between former adversaries with historical grievances when empires are to be won and maintained. This happens when prophet-sharing entities bury the hatchet because the collapse of meaning, God, and the pursuit of endless empire makes the usual strife seem like a catastrophe already arrived.

Like a hurricane on land that is gaining rather than losing strength, the prophets cannot afford the divisions that led to previous catastrophes in history. Often previous catastrophes fuel the hurricane, making it stronger when it should be weakening.

Negotiating the Prophetic

Nonetheless, the prophetic next step is far from obvious. Imagining Star of David Helicopter Gunships in the Ark of the Covenant is one thing. Surviving them, then flourishing, is another.

The prophetic strides on colonized space; our geographic location, broadly considered, is important. Jews, Christians, and Muslims may be one faith in the end. Maybe not. The boundary-crossing prophets are hardly free of limitations, even when the prophetic wildcard is in play. Nonetheless, the prophet has to be careful lest scholarly nuance, itself a politics, diminishes the prophetic voice.

Disciplining the prophetic comes in many formulations, including the politically correct progressive ones. It seems that sidelining the prophetic in service to other concerns, some of them quite worthwhile in and of themselves, is the academic order of the day. Religion's order of the day and political orders of the day, too. The world conspires to bury the prophetic. Discernment is key, even as the prophet remains focused.

Though the prophet is called in the present, memory remains the anchor. Prophet-sharing is one thing, intersectional analysis another. When the prophetic is over scrutinized, it falters. Overthinking tires the legs of the prophet. For Jews, though, who are not grafted on like Christians or confronted with the close of the prophetic like Muslims, the evolution of the prophetic, always needed, happens as the chips fall.

The prophetic voice is always on the road in one form or another, training like a fighter. Even when sitting cross-legged on a cushion, the prophet prepares for a deeper asceticism. The prophet's foray into the realm of happiness is, at times, devoutly wished for. Everyone deserves moments when the planets align in one's favor. Then, when the other shoe drops, as it is bound to do, the prophet is ready for the next round.

Happiness within exile. Perhaps there is a better word than happiness. Like love, the definition is important and contested. When you dissect the meaning of happiness or love you are left with immense questions, partial answers, and more unknowns than you start with. More or less like prophet and prophetic, happiness and love are easier if you just let it flow. Still, we crave definitions. With time, whatever definitions we arrive at dissipate anyway. Happiness and love, again like the prophetic, are the journey toward. Arrival is rarely in the cards even if an offered definition is accepted as valid.

So why begin at the end, with answers before the journey commences? Perhaps to assuage anxiety, to stabilize the demonstrably unstable, like defining God, covenant, messiah, salvation. All fine and good if we really knew what we are signing on to. Perhaps this is this why religious creedal announcements often become more and more militant as the anxiety about their truthfulness grows.

What we are supposed to believe in, what we must believe in, we often don't. Incorrect answers and no-go areas are defined. In order to be transgressed? Instead, it is better to simply live and let these important questions remain open, even as we make decisions, plant our feet and put one foot ahead of the other. Perhaps, when all is said and done, practicing an asceticism that is open to happiness and love and the prophetic is easier.

Instead, happiness, love, and the prophetic seem separated by an ocean. One has to travel a long, long way to get from here to there. Think of the ocean before airplanes, before ocean liners, and you begin to get a sense of the gulf between one and the other. The dark interiors of the prophetic haunt the prophet as much as the prophet haunts power.

The light of happiness and love, if they cross the prophet's path, is momentary. The prophet is enthralled by the surprise and grateful; he has to see and record it all before nightfall, again before dawn, and at times during the midday hours. Because shutting down the prophetic is likewise momentary. It is the challenge of challenges whether the prophetic and love can co-exist over time, challenging and nurturing each other.

The prophet fears she will become lost in love. The asceticism is so ingrained—inscribed?—that the prophet fears her vocation will be taken away, in a sense, stolen away, like a thief in the night. Upon waking will the prophetic have fled? For the prophet failure

Negotiating the Prophetic

is understood. It is part and parcel of the prophet's asceticism. Love, indeed happiness, seems destined for others, even when offered freely.

The prophet is dubious, on guard, an agnostic on love and happiness. Gratitude is another thing altogether, within the prophet's asceticism, to be struggled for, gained and lost, to be glimpsed in partial justice achieved, in the beauty of others, and the wonders of creation. In a final sense, can the prophet be grateful for his prophetic vocation, even if the prophet knows it has been given, coming, if not from God, then from Somewhere Else?

To take root, happiness and love have to come within the prophetic. Both have to travel beside and accompany the prophet, allowing the dark interiors of the prophet and moments of illumination to have its space and rhythms. For the prophet lives through the collapse of meaning and God in and outside of colonial space and even within the colonial spaces of the prophetic. Can we imagine the prophets happy and in love without considering that the prophet has his own demons to fight?

The prophet for others, how she is perceived. The prophet for herself, how she sees herself. When things look the same from outside and inside. When they don't. The marvel of the prophet, as others know her. The aloneness of the prophet. Is that aloneness somehow shared?

Traveling in colonial spaces, life on the ropes, is such a path open to life abundant? The prophet sees the landscape, feels its contours. Elucidation through abundance? The prophets' lives, are they the same, even if they come from foreign shores? The difficulties are so great within Jewish life, the prophet's hope for happiness may be found among the Other Nations. Yet the Other Nations, biblically-speaking, and all through Jewish history, are the signpost of being lost, without a destiny, assimilating to a world without the God of Israel, (un)chosen. Now, in the collapse, dwelling in the abyss of injustice, is that ultimate divide being overcome?

The spiral downward of the chosen ones is obvious. Now a permanent condition, without hope of return, Israel, the state, may itself become an Other Nation. Normative Jewishness, the Jewish establishment and beyond, as an Other Nation. Prophetic Jews on the margins of both, yet dwelling within the Other Nations. Is there a place where Jews of Conscience can lay their head without the drumbeat of justice denied beating throughout the night? The trauma of collective Israel going AWOL, permanently. Is the exile of Jews of Conscience the last exile in Jewish history, there being nowhere else to go?

The Jewish prophetic is being boxed into the corner, fists flying at her, the life of the people Israel flashing before her glazed eyes. How to survive the onslaught? How can the prophet flee the corner, emerge in another part of the ring, right herself and live for another round? Yet knowing that survival is dicey, that another onslaught awaits, a moment's respite is needed, wanted, hoped for, even if this, too, if achieved, is only temporary.

So the Jewish prophets commune with the Other Nations, themselves divided by empire between and within them, a *novum* in Jewish history. The Jewish prophets choosing between and among the Other Nations, fraught with symbolism, a form of resistance. Where to travel, where to identify, where to live? Life's questions multiply.

Once decided, is it time to set down roots with and among others or will the Jewish prophets of our day find a way to set themselves apart in exile? Being set apart might be ego. Being set apart might be tradition. Being set apart might be destiny. Being set apart might be fidelity. Being set apart might be an illusion.

All of the above, perhaps with, no doubt, a touch of nostalgia for the God That Was and for the covenant that was. Living after, now with others who are also living after what has happened in their history. *After* this and that historical catastrophe, betrayal, assimilation to empire, resistance to empire, whether the empire of another community or the empire within, it seems everyone has been there and done that.

Will there be a time after the Other Nations when there is no Other? And realizing that in our modern landscape Others abound, but stripped of the protective layer that even a persecuted Other once provided within community, crossing boundaries are

Negotiating the Prophetic

the Prophets Of All Nations coming into solidarity with the new Destitute Other? The Prophetic Other in defense of the Destitute Other?

Shared prophets. Within all the nations/peoples/communities, the Destitute Other inhabits the same globe that the Prophets Of All Nations inhabit. No need for names, just the gathering of everyone who wants another way. Easy it seems, just unite and conquer the Elite Of All Nations that divides and conquers. Why dally over historical traditions, divisions created along history's byways, identities that are compromised and shattered beyond repair? Why try to redeem the irredeemable, when, even if redeemed, the Destitute Other will continue to grow?

The hope, if we recover the true impetus of our traditions all will be well. Even if those who stray quit their addiction to power over others, their return would be less to the origins than to a future newly dressed in the garments of the old. The old cannot be brought back to life, even if it was as we want to imagine it, which it wasn't anyway. Like a hoped-for return to childhood, the moment passes and we are where we are, in midlife or beyond, with trauma, yes, and learning, if we're lucky a certain wisdom. Early Israel, early Christianity, early Islam, early modernity, these religious movements should be studied and mined for insights. Recreated? Not a chance. Not even to be wished for.

The prophetic is hardly possible without these wayward histories, traditions, symbols, so entangled with injustice and atrocity. The prophetic as pure, as innocent, is a dead-end. With such thoughts the prophet ventures beyond negotiation into the apocalyptic. Yet the apocalyptic is too self-involved, too harsh and too simplistic. It asks of religion, society and the individual more than they can deliver.

The prophets need deep reservoirs to draw from to keep them grounded. Symbols, movements, destinies, martyrs, justice seekers, along with a knowledge of how corrupted each can be, is essential. The prophetic is about bringing the powerful to justice and much, much more. Though justice can be achieved in some cases, over time other injustices will take their place. Institutions, too, some of them, over time, make the justice transition, in partial terms.

Appealing to the old, embracing the shattered symbols requires a different focus. What we have, we have, however flawed, there is meaning in that they exist, have been struggled over and through. They are signposts on the human journey with their own pilgrimage, which we are taking up anew.

Christian symbols: Conquistador's Cross, Dietrich Bonhoeffer's Cross, Archbishop Oscar Romero's Cross, same Cross, different meaning? Even Bonhoeffer's "arcane discipline" he wrote about in prison before his execution needs some symbol. Jewish narrative: the Holocaust dead, Israeli power. Same narrative, different meaning?

Though transformation must occur, the abandonment of what is prophetically meaningful is dangerous. Empty of history and symbols, if that is possible, where would life's meaning be represented? Even the disputes, rebellions and denials of these very same symbols have a lasting effect on history.

The deep reservoir prophets need is the same reservoir all of us need. Therefore what the prophets carry with them is as compromised, impure and degraded as the prophets are. The prophets live in the same history and drink the same water as everyone else, as it must be. Resources are scarce. The prophets and the prophetic drink from many wells.

Is everything prophetic local? Though there is a universal dimension to prophetic thought and action, as the slogan goes, think globally, act locally. This makes sense, especially when the indigenous is factored in. Obviously, it depends what global, local and indigenous mean, since definitions vary widely.

On the Jewish side of prophet-sharing this is a problem area. Though Jews are heavily invested in the state of Israel, at least conceptually, the indigenous of Jewish is the prophetic. And though local to Jewish history, the Jewish prophetic. has spread wherever Jews have roamed and wherever Christianity and Islam have found a home. Then there are those influenced by the Jewish prophetic

Negotiating the Prophetic

outside the monotheistic faiths. The Jewish prophetic is only as local and as universal as conceptual frameworks can be.

Few in the world are untouched by the Jewish prophetic gone global. Nonetheless, the prophetic's specifically Jewish manifestation remains distinctive. It is hard to believe that even with prophet-sharing the distinctive dimension of the Jewish indigenous prophetic around the world, or the prophetic in general, would be better off if the Jewish prophetic lost its moorings. Prophet-sharing is less a blending than an authentic offering of the diverse soils that the prophetic has taken root within. The one foundational root, the indigenous Jewish prophetic, even as it mixes and matches with the prophetic of the Other Nations, needs protection and nourishment.

4

Our Prophetic Future

There are losses and gains in the ever-evolving prophetic tradition. Tradition, the distortion of which being part of the problem, is nevertheless essential. All traditions apply the brakes to innovation. How far can the prophet stray from tradition before the prophetic runs dry, journeys somewhere else, and embarks on a future without a home? Yet the very reading of the tradition under religion's often unhelpful gaze, with its unceasing religious and academic study, sheer repetition and use for every competing cause in the world, including for the building of empire, weighs down the prophetic.

Even the repeated calls for justice made legitimate by reference to the prophetic tradition are too often literal, quoting the prophets, using the prophets as set pieces, as if nothing has changed in our universe and everything that transpired in ancient times happened as the Bible tells us. Even when the prophetic agrees with a specific political and economic cause, the theatrics are too well-timed. Our prophetic backdrop needs updating. The prophetic tradition needs a fresh coat of paint—only?

The challenges before us augur a new prophetic that, on the one hand, has lost almost everything and, on the other, has little to gain. It is less about the prophetic gaining the world and losing its soul, an always relevant religious aphorism, or the prophetic on the threshhold of succeeding and regaining its soul, as if the prophetic is on the verge of success. Our historical situation is too dire for these aphorisms.

The prophetic is losing on all accounts; even its traditional marginal position is eroding. For the biblical prophets were at least recognized by the people and by the powerful as possibly from God. If from God, their power was assumed, whether they experienced that power or not. The prophets have no recognized claim to that authority today from others or even themselves. Whether you decry or support the prophets, everyone knows they are on their own.

In biblical times, the stakes in the struggle between empire and the prophetic were more than victory or defeat. The struggle involved divine attribution and protection. Israel's destiny was on the line. The entire world was at stake. Without romanticizing and whatever its historicity, the Bible is a high stakes adventure.

In our time narratives of meaning and destiny are fractured and shattered, if they remain at all. What matters are the latest employment statistics and stock market fluctuations. The fear of change, even of contesting economic and political systems, is too much to bear for populations totally dependent on endless consumption, global tourism and a relentless search for the material resources that might eventually destroy us.

Today pundits thrive, the prophets largely go unrecognized. For the most part prophets are seen and often see themselves as activists. Though the biblical prophets were active, activism is an inadequate view of their life. The danger of endless activism is that it can become activity for its own sake. Moving from cause to cause, all laudable, activism becomes a way of life, a calling card and sometimes an addiction. Spiritually-oriented activists are hardly above the fray but have it right in their insistence that the impetus for solidarity comes from somewhere other than itself.

If justice is achieved, if justice is ever achieved—only—we are still left with the ultimate question of meaning. And since justice won't be achieved or, if achieved here, will be lacking somewhere else, justice for justice sake is empty. The biblical prophets never go justice—only. The biblical prophets never go God—only. With all their certainty and vulnerability, the peculiar mix of justice and God, the prophets rarely lapse into action without a meaning within and beyond the act itself. Thus the question: Does the collapse of meaning and God further impoverish our already difficult activity on behalf of justice?

There is the risk that prophetic hope, always under duress, will wither. How many returns to God have there been in history without justice being attained? There are some who caution against believing in God before justice is established. If and when justice arrives we will see God face to face. Or perhaps if justice arrives we will see each other face to face in a new way, deeply, as if for the first time. Will that be like seeing the face of God? Is seeing ourselves, our true being, a risk worth taking? For face to face, seeing ourselves as we are, is the true leap of faith. Can we survive seeing and being seen, thus ourselves and others being naked before the world?

Perhaps this is why we build walls that divide us. Supposedly a hope for unity beyond walls, religions divide us as well. Even our worship of God is divided between us and them, the saved of one faith, the (un)saved of another. Are the divisions so strong because we know we are both saved and (un)saved? The prophetic cannot bring down the barriers between us and them or within ourselves with the wave of her hand, proclaiming God and humanity as now joined.

Even God needs distance from God, lest God see himself face to face and come up wanting. The God of Israel is too unstable, mercurial, reflective and flawed to countenance a full viewing or self-accounting. Perhaps God has not and does not want to find the justice formula. For if God did find the justice formula and implement it, the danger is that God would become manifest and transparent. Thus vulnerable?

Our Prophetic Future

Making God exist is religion's self-assigned job. It is religion's greatest failure. The more religion works on making God exist, the more glaring the failure and the more violence religion serves up or blesses. In turn, religion becomes more and more discredited. Until religion's collapse becomes the conduit for a God who might one day be glimpsed? The task of making God exist is the work of our lives and may be the mirage of mirages. Unless the I AM is the one who loves the prophets. Full stop, as in, I AM WHO LOVES THE PROPHETS.

An evangelical turning with a twist, perhaps, reorienting our sensibilities about justice and God. If God fails to love, and in a special way, the prophets, what kind of God is God? Perhaps God already exists in and through the prophets, the prophets preparing the way for another perception of what God is and isn't. God's preferential love for those who do God's bidding on earth is startling.

I AM WHO LOVES THE PROPHETS—within the collapse. Do the prophets in exile hear this voice breaking through? Without verification, it is hard being a Jew in exile. A Jew in exile without God is doubly difficult. Impossible?

The task of making God exist, that task being justice and meaning, is an ongoing process. That justice is more and more urgent, is seemingly eternally delayed, yet a calling that persists, like the prophets themselves, one that makes the prophet's already high stakes higher. The prophets do keep on, coming from Somewhere Else? Does God love in the love we show one another, a Christian formulation most often honored in the breach? Yet that too remains within the task of making justice exist, with or without the (premature?) naming of I AM.

God and justice is that peculiar combination that liberated and haunted ancient Israel. Creative conjunction it was. Israel's invention? To separate ancient Israel's history between real and imagined is a task itself. Regardless of the historicity of the Exodus and beyond, ancient Israel bequeathed the prophetic to the world. A greater and more disturbing gift is difficult to imagine and, besides, imagination takes flight from something. Therefore the prophetic is within history forever. Like Israel's real or imagined God.

Studying origins as history is important, though, with all its complexity, limiting. Studying origins within the here and now can promote an expanding view. If ancient Israel's gift is the prophetic, what is ours? The best we can offer, and what an offering it is, is to marvel at the prophetic's Jewish texture, expand the prophetic view by exploring the texture of its global sensibility, and see where the persistent prophetic leads us. For the instability of ancient Israel's prophetic is for all of us.

Like theology, instability is contextual. But as in theology, instability has an essential ingredient. Even in collapse, justice and God remain linked. The prophets of our day have to think this connection of justice and God within collapse, then articulate what can and cannot be said about both. At the outset, it seems that justice is easier to articulate than God. Upon further reflection we see that justice is easier to articulate only when it remains conceptual. Like God? However, the devil is in the justice and God details. In the details, neither justice nor God are easy or, at times, possible.

Some of the time we imagine God existing. Other times we continue on as if God does not exist. Is it our responsibility to make God exist? If anything can attest to God's existence, justice can. Even, then, justice can only lay the groundwork for another attempt at God. This, through language and, perhaps, mostly through silence.

To get to the root of God it may be best to spare the hymns, the creeds, and the always selectively read and barely understood scriptures that call us to prayer, action, and belief in God. Religious artifacts have their place for those religiously inclined in a certain way. There is a danger here as well, for these same religious may eventually place those so inclined outside the religious community's gate.

Do some have access to a higher power than others do? Or are we in the same leaky boat, struggling to keep afloat and find shore before the ultimate darkness descends? Light is found in the darkest of places by those who know little about God and those who know more. When committed to justice, perhaps a discerning agnosticism is best—being suspicious of all-God and of no-God, finding meaning and lack of meaning, hoping for justice around the corner and believing in no-justice ever, celebrating times when the beauty of life suggests God contradicted by times when the ugliness of life prevails. One is a believer or a non-believer by the place one ends up most frequently. Theism and atheism are rarely polar opposites. Both are present in the Other. After.

JEWISH PROPHETIC AFTERLIFE

After it is. After, then after, then after once again. There are so many afters in history and in our own lives that the parade of afters could drive us to despair. When the afters point to the absurdity of the world, our strivings and even our negations, our alternatives diminish. Yet, perhaps counter-intuitively, in the afters, life exists in the present.

Life after, afterlife, is the life we didn't expect, wasn't predicted, wildcard life that only afters can bring. Often our afterlife is too small to notice, especially if we are primarily involved in the meta-meanings of our world. When the prophetic hits the meta-meanings wall hard the only way forward is to dwell in what remains.

Lament it is and, though, so necessary in life, lament can become a stumbling block when it becomes all-encompassing. The danger is that the prophet and the prophetic can become stuck in their own dire vision which, though often accurate, is rarely the entire story. Since, as the prophets, life keeps coming, persists and, once in a while, when we least expect it, takes us by surprise, being open to a future is essential. The prophet and the prophetic have to keep their ears to the ground and their eyes wide open. Searching for light.

Light in the darkness, a cliché too often employed. Another cliché: What doesn't kill you makes you stronger. There is truth in both and the prophetic goes there at times. Even prophets need solace. But the human journey moves beyond cliché certainties. When the public spotlight dims, the interior world of the prophet goes dark. Clichés do little here and may even be hurtful. Like being called a prophet, then being served up the clichés about prophets never being accepted or embraced in their time or at home.

Being labeled a prophet separates you from others, mostly as an excuse for the deliverer of the cliché. The prophet is not an excuse for others to excuse themselves from the field of battle. The exile of the prophet, her separation even from admirers, is true enough. No prophet accepts this state of affairs. The prophet thinks that the prophetic is within all of us. He wonders why in God's name his admirer is absent on the field of battle.

The prophet does not arrive to redeem theology or to renew religious tradition. Priests, ministers, imams, and rabbis try their hands at this. Most often the prophet is against the grain of the religiosity she grew up with. For some unexplained reason the prophet enters the tradition differently. As was originally intended? If not, sometimes against the tradition's intention. Imagining conscience, then practicing it, the prophet frees herself of the religious tradition and even from the prophetic tradition, at least as both are handed down.

Clichés about the prophets must be abandoned, both by those who want to distance themselves from the prophetic and by those who seek to draw near and embrace the prophetic. Being lauded as a prophet is as much a death for the prophet as being decried. The prophet runs away from his admirers as fast as he runs from his detractors, lest the prophet become stuck in another's gaze. Those who spend a lifetime studying the prophets, who mine them for their audacity and wisdom, as well as those who endlessly monitor the prophets to discipline them, both should beware. The prophets rarely fit into their neat little boxes and, if they do for a moment or two, soon, just like that, they're Somewhere Else.

Another lesson for the prophets and the prophetic community is to beware of being used for someone else's agenda. Those who try to use and abuse the prophets should be warned. Another cliché? Is there a final arbiter of the prophetic, one with the power to punish? The question remains whether the fuss over the prophet is worth the energy. Since the prophets have little or no power, why bother with them?

Especially in our time, the fierce attention paid to the prophets is the riddle of riddles. Why pay attention to the prophet's words, when even the possibility of them becoming an expansion of the old or creating a new scripture are dubious? For God's sake, don't the powerful realize that the prophet who knows all is lost, is lost herself? In the virtual world, the words of the prophet, her justice-seeking and lament, may flash across a screen or two. To what effect?

There are at least two dimensions to the prophet, the first, the prophet in the public square, the second, the prophet at home with himself. It would be another useless cliché to say that the prophet, so intent and focused, is above the adulation and critique she receives. Especially the critique, since the prophet's supporters think that for the prophet the high, above-it-all road, is a no-brainer. Such a high-minded ethical model the prophet is, legions above the pettiness of life in the public square!

The prophet's cliché admirers are on the wrong track, for an unexpected aspect of the prophet is pettiness. Though this often goes unnoticed or without remark, the prophet has to guard his public personae and sometimes, to do so, has to strike an opponent beneath the belt. The pettiness found among the biblical prophets is remarkable in its display, and in our day, within the collapse of meaning and God, the prophet's vulnerability increases. Over the long run, vulnerability without pettiness is a forced deception.

If we imagine the prophet fierce and silent, we must also imagine the prophet taking slights to heart and striking back. For to be above it all renders the prophet other worldly. It diminishes the prophet's instability and, thus, her disturbing presence. However the prophet presents himself, the prophet is far from the bourgeois ideal. Even if he lives in house with a picket fence.

Presence it is, the prophet and the prophetic community appearing and reappearing through Jewish history and now across the globe in different forms. The persistence of the prophetic throughout history is as much its message as its success or failure.

Finding Our Voice

In fact, failure might be the key to the prophetic, again tacking against the activist's wind. While failing is hardly the prophet's goal, failure of the prophetic is as persistent as the prophetic itself. Meaning that the prophetic message in the bottle washes up on every shore, often when it is least expected, and thus the shoreline is never fully secure.

If the failure of the prophet is so obvious and predictable, why, then, send out search parties when the prophetic presence is announced? And in our time when we are unable to claim God boldly, if at all, so that the power from above has been removed, for the worldly powers to send out search-and-destroy forces seems silly. Is this desire to murder the prophet an ancient, out-of-date, knee-jerk reaction on the part of the powerful? Or is it a realization by the powerful that the prophetic voice is now ingrained in the human psyche, without need of permission or divine authority to guide it?

Do the biblical prophets think the people Israel are the promised ones of God? Yes, decisively. Do the contemporary Jewish prophets think that Jews are the promised ones of God? Yes, with a proviso. But before coming to the complications, the following should be stated in simple terms: No one who sacrifices for others or who believes that history has a moral dimension is wholly without an inscribed communal sensibility; No one who sacrifices on behalf of others and relates that sacrifice to history is without a beginning that formed and calls them.

For Jews it is the tradition of traditions that there is something special about being Jewish. Nowhere is Jewish history narrated without that specialness. Whether or not Jews are special, if truth in this area can be established, is beside the point. Jews have always believed themselves special. You cannot be Jewish without that sense of specialness and this is true especially when Jews go out of their way to deny it.

Why deny so vociferously what can hardly be broached in our post-modern sensibility where everyone everywhere is alike, at least in theory? Because in modernity there is a minority of the world's population who believe they are the chosen ones? In fact, other minorities, including the politically powerful and moneyed elites who believe they deserve to be served by others, believe they are chosen as well. Modernity's concept of chosenness is dumbed down.

In the biblical narrative, chosenness links justice and God. With the guidance of the God of Liberation, Israel's destiny is to build a new social order of justice, peace and compassion. The prophets are called first and foremost to remind Israel of why God chose Israel. The penalties for recreating the empire structures God led Israel out of are extreme. When Israel turns its back on God, that is the justice and destiny announced through the prophets, God goes scorched earth.

So, yes, chosenness is an issue, assumed and announced by the biblical prophets, assumed and unannounced by prophetic Jews today. More, the unannounced is explicitly denied by Jews on the frontlines today. There's hardly a choice in the matter since particularity and essence are no-go areas in today's justice movements. Such sentiments are viewed as retrograde affirmations reserved for the unjust elites who seek to make the world over in their image.

Why, then, the increasing centrality of Israel-Palestine to prophetic Jews? There are many unjust situations in the world, why pick Israel-Palestine to concentrate on if one's ties to Jewish identity are diminished or rejected? The vehement dismissal of chosenness is too neat, too predictable, too avant-garde. Is Jewish concentration on Israel-Palestine a last ditch effort to stop Jews from their final assimilation to unjust power?

The prophets are self-absorbed. Except for God's commission, Israel's destiny is all they have. As a package deal, the prophet cannot have one without the other. The biblical prophets have no choice. Called by God to lecture, cajole and plead with Israel, God's chosen are obvious in their adherence to God and in their transgressions against God. Yet notice that the biblical prophets have reason to doubt both. God calls them directly but, over time God is sometimes there, other times not. God is an undependable commander. In its obedience, Israel is doubtful.

Finding Our Voice

On the best of days, Israel, as a virtually unknown and unspectacular people, is a peculiar choice for such an exalted destiny. So it must seem to the prophets. Small signs are there; they flash across the biblical texts. The true signs of the times, in bold letters, is that Israel is going down. In spite of God's commands, Israel's injustice and arrogance defies the prophet's imagination. What was God thinking? What is God thinking? For the prophets, God and Israel's chosenness is the dead-end of dead-ends.

The biblical prophets persist. The persistence of the prophets, who come after God ceases to command, take up their stubbornness. To persist is as difficult as it was to accept God's mission which, often obvious at the start, in the end spells doom. The prophets are continually on the line. So, too, Israel. God is on the line as well. For if Israel and the prophets fail, where that leaves God is an open question.

We can only speculate what it means for God to dwell without Israel and the prophets. Once together, they are joined at the hip. This, because God is involved in the world and for some reason needs the world to validate his existence. So God needs Israel. God needs the prophets. Though seemingly self-sufficient, God's name cannot be known in the world without Israel and the prophets. Yet both let God down. Despite it all, Israel, the prophets, and God persist.

At times the biblical prophets have such beatific visions it brings tears to the reader's eyes. The other side of the prophetic vision, the violent and the tragic, is equally powerful but dire. Tears are of a different order. Israel's injustice and unrepentant stubbornness causes chastisement without end. On occasion, God adopts a scorched earth policy.

One wonders if God and the prophets know their predicted destiny for an unrepentant Israel is over-the-top, way too harsh from any point of view and counter-productive to boot. Their disappointment is magnified when God and the prophets appear almost insane in their anger. For any reason scorched earth is insane, has to be struggled against, conscience being the first barrier. That God and the prophets leap over conscience without looking back is a harsh indictment. Should we repudiate God and the prophets for such a leap?

Perhaps the biblical prophets should have invoked conscience more frequently. The prophet's remorse about Israel's treatment is infrequent. Introspection is rarely at the center of the prophet's reflections. The prophets infrequently call themselves to account. God is low on repentance. Without approving of Israel's wayward behavior, it remains that God and the prophets are too hard on Israel. Neither allow Israel to behave as the Other Nations do, though mostly Israel behaves exactly like them.

The biblical prophets are the conscience of Israel. Yet throughout history nations rarely consult their conscience and, when they do, it is mostly self-interested and rhetorical. Such accounting is limited and only partially honest. Israel, on the other hand, knows it cannot sign and deliver its own bill of sale. Even as it tries, Israel is aware of the God/prophet tribunal already in session. This constant scrutiny is a trauma. What nation, whatever its destiny, can survive such judgment? Israel does and doesn't survive, at least for periods of time. Nonetheless, even in exile, like the prophets and God, Israel persists.

The persistence of the prophet. Even the shattered light she gathers is extraordinary. The light the prophet finds in the darkness is suffused with a destiny always a step away from our grasp and, paradoxically, right within reach. With the stakes so high, at every moment, and with the collapse so obvious, without being the last word, even the threatened scorched earth offers hope.

Though now, with the return of Jews to modern day Israel complete, return itself takes on a new meaning and introduces yet another level to the prophetic journey. For return now can only mean the challenge of an ethical life where more light can be found—a life with others. Return now can only mean an entry into the New Diaspora, with exiles from every continent and religion— a life with others.

As the state of Israel oppresses Palestinians and assists Arab nations to oppress their own people, the cycle of violence and atrocity continues. This permanent feature of Jewish life forbids a renewed life in the New Diaspora as if Jewish life is only there, as if the future of Jewish life in the New Diaspora is a return to innocence. Whatever happens to Jewish life among the diverse exiles in the New Diaspora, the state of Israel will remain the Jewish ethical battlefield. Should Israel then be abandoned as—only—a colonial venture that has hijacked Jewish life to the point where Israel must be dissolved totally and, in one way or another, vanish?

The Jewish return to Israel is now readjusted. The cycle of entering the land, then and now, has come full circle with a homeland for Jews for all practical purposes being defeated by the state that claims it all, much like religions that claim God as their very own. The distance needed from these claims being what ancient Israel named idolatry. After all, the very concept of idolatry means that naming God is a dangerous adventure. So, too, with every state, including Israel.

"Not in Our Name," dissenting Jews chant. For some the violence perpetrated by the state of Israel render impossible the very idea of a Jewish state. This would mean that exile is perpetual, part of the Jewish essence. Perhaps exile, like the prophetic, is indigenous to Jewish life. This presumes that the New Diaspora cannot become a homecoming for Jews of all stripes, including prophetic Jews. Can being with others, permanently, as one among others, without a special calling and with a stability rarely experienced in Jewish history, especially over time, be found by Jews? So that Jews are seen by others as ordinary and Jews will see themselves as ordinary?

Ordinary Jews. Well, of course, Jews are quite ordinary. Being ordinary as human beings is a given. All have other dimensions as well. At least in capability and under certain circumstances, all can rise to the occasion. We are extra-ordinary for stretches of time. The extra-ordinary moments are our human wildcard. The extra-ordinary part of us is related to our own development, yet always within a broader and specific context, for example, in African American history. Martin Luther King Jr., was extra-ordinary because of his individual talents, within the broader arc of Black history. King rose to the occasion in the context of his people's history. Without that history, King would have been a successful minister and writer. He would not have become the iconic prophetic presence he ultimately became.

PROPHETIC REMNANTS

The extra-ordinary has roots, deep ones, that certain individuals are nurtured within and can draw upon. "Jewish" has its own distinctives to draw upon. A history whose essential thrust is the prophetic, with a sense of a special destiny, is unable to exist over the long haul if those roots are cut back or displaced. Most of Jewish history existed without a state. Noted. However, the anticipation of Jerusalem and return, in its various interpretations, remained.

After the latest return of Jews to Israel, a return which ultimately gave birth to the contemporary exile of prophetic Jews, Jews face an internal struggle that remains within the traditional Jewish framework. Hence the question: Is the wholesale revolt against all aspects of the Jewish tradition only possible because the traditional framework remains inscribed in Jewish life?

The traditional framework of Jewish life, marked by the rabbis, is awash with fascinating religious interpretations, historical detours, and mundane details of everyday life. The Rabbinic Era formed mostly after the expulsion of Jews from first century Palestine by the Romans and within the remnant of Jews that remained. The attempts of the rabbis to give meaning to Jewish life after this catastrophe were gathered first in the Palestinian and Babylonian Talmuds, then endlessly debated and refined until the Holocaust and the formation of the state of Israel. Now empowered in Israel and America but without mentioning the tangled history in the state of Israel, the rabbinic mode more of less leads to statements such as in the introduction to *The Jewish Bible Study*: "With the canonization of God's revelation in the form of the written books of the Bible, new revelations through prophets became superfluous. Prophecy was gradually replaced by scriptural study and interpretation, and prophets by scribes, sages and rabbis."

Finding Our Voice

What is the author of these comments thinking? Both the Holocaust and the state of Israel are formative events in Jewish history akin to the exile from Palestine in the first century. These events need interpretation, too, and perhaps lead to new revelations that can only come from the prophets of our day. For Jews of Conscience, scriptural study and interpretation of texts, scribes, sages, and rabbis, have failed. More, what once was revolutionary in the rabbinic interpretative framework is now used to deflect, deny and bury the very prophetic voices Jews and Palestinians need so desperately.

Nonetheless, the rabbinic framework has its place, as a past which can, when directed properly, point a way for the embodied prophetic to deepen its indigenous impulses. For the most part, the rabbinic has become a series of empty interpretations that deflect the pressing issues facing the Jewish people. This hardly means the rabbis were always empty sloganeers, far from it. Unfortunately, our contemporary rabbis deserve this appellation. After all, with few exceptions, most rabbis choose ignorance about what has and is happening to Palestinians. In turn, they pedal ignorance to their congregations.

A transformed rabbinate, however, would give a tremendous boost to a Jewishly engaged prophetic. Even the New Age Jewish spirituality that freely and often colonially borrows from Buddhism and Native American spirituality can have its own room in a prophetically renovated Jewishness. As long as both see their lifeline as borrowed time and in service to the naked and unadorned prophetic. In the meantime, they may function as a way for the Jewish prophetic to catch its breath after years and decades on the field of battle. The problem is that too often, even in the most progressive settings, rabbinic and New Age spirituality become platforms for the Jewish equivalent of church planting. Charismatic rabbis, sometimes self-ordained, fend off the prophetic that claims, quite correctly, that the dressing up of the prophetic itself is a form of idolatry.

Can anyone authentically canonize God's revelation as our *Jewish Study Bible* author asserts has already been done? What

Our Prophetic Future

might such a canonization mean other than assimilation to unjust power? Distance from God such a canonization ensures is the very occasion for the Jewish prophetic to reappear in full force. Do the rabbis realize they are playing with prophetic fire?

Years ago there was a study that analyzed why rabbis die relatively young. The report concluded that rabbis die younger than the norm because they are caught between their congregation's need to place them on a pedestal and the congregation's need to push them off that pedestal. In sum, congregations want their rabbis to be holier than they are and also resent them for being so. The tug is too much for the rabbi's heart and soul, thus the rabbi's early earthly exit.

What if the death of the rabbi and her congregation's ambivalence have more to do with the contradiction of the headlong rush for Jews to be normal, stable and prosperous, thus clashing with the inevitable prophetic that haunts Jewish life? What if the suppression of the indigenous Jewish prophetic is the dis-ease that starts the ill-health of the rabbi and, in another way, with her congregation as well?

Rabbis, aside, those who wrote the deepest and most penetrating theologies about the Holocaust and what it means for Jews and the world today have lived long lives. The major Holocaust theologians have lived into their seventies and eighties. They have prospered, too, writing about the Holocaust darkness, yes, and profoundly so, but also becoming cheerleaders for the state of Israel, insisting that Israel and its empowerment is the modern litmus test for Jewishness. In their view, breaking with Israel or criticizing it too vociferously is tantamount to blasphemy.

Holocaust theologians laid out the redline of contemporary Jewish life with attendant penalties, the most stringent being excommunication from the Jewish community. On God, Holocaust theologians are very close to the Jewish prophets of our day. They, too, see God as absent, AWOL at Auschwitz. Regardless, Jews, like others, need some kind of transcendent certainty and, in a strange transposition, the Holocaust became that transcendence. As did Israel. This elevation of the Holocaust and Israel to almost transcendent categories was bound to stir the prophets eventually. For Holocaust/Israel religiosity has become a cover for a multitude of sins, first among them being injustice.

One encounters the Holocaust as transcendent in the United States Holocaust Memorial Museum in Washington, DC. The private capital expenditures for the museum were tremendous and the government's role in its placement near the hallowed ground of America's monuments is telling. Jews have made it in America. Though Jews were on their way in America before the Holocaust and, especially after World War II ended, it was the Holocaust story that sealed the Jewish deal with America and, eventually, America's deal with Israel. This happened in the wake of the 1967 Arab-Israeli war, which Israel won decisively.

In America, commemorating the Holocaust and honoring Israel's victory ushered in a Golden Age for Jews, where upward mobility in all areas of American life was achieved. Thus the ultimate refusal of the Jewish prophetic buy-in is all the more startling. For though in the past Jewish prophetic critique of American exceptionality was strong, the Holocaust and Israel became a stumbling block for many years. Holocaust consciousness was strong and becoming stronger. The prophets breathed on the margins. Then the margins became smaller and smaller; Jewish life was hanging on a the edge of a precipice. Interest in making it in America and a strong Israel raised an important question: Especially after the Holocaust and with an embattled Israel, doesn't Jewish survival take precedence over the prophetic?

Though battered by the resurgence of the Jewish prophetic that is critical of the use of the Holocaust to justify oppression of Palestinians, the Holocaust/Israel axis remains. The notion that Jews are innocent in suffering and empowerment is over. No community or state is innocent in their empowerment. Having lost the narrative of innocence, Israel, with the assistance of the Jewish establishment in America, now uses naked power to overcome their loss of support. Ethical issues are front and center but practical issues haunt this power as well. What happens to Jews inside and

Our Prophetic Future

outside Israel if and when that power is stripped away? Without innocence and power, where will Jews be?

A material rather than mythic reading of history is crucial here as well as exploration of elements of Jewish identity. Who are Jews when only naked power is their shield? Those primarily concerned about the continuation of Jewish life are worried about what will become of Jewishness without the Holocaust and Israel as the anchor of Jewish identity. This may be why uncritical loyalty to the Holocaust and Israel is so important to maintain.

After the Holocaust and Israel diminish in their importance will there be anything left of "Jewish"? Now that the Holocaust and Israel have dominated Jewish life for so many decades the issue is significant. Yet the Jewish prophetic voice is less interested in a Jewish future, especially if that Jewish future is dominated by unjust power. The concern of the Jewish prophetic in our time is the Jewish assimilation to unjust power.

For in the eyes of the Jewish prophetic, Jewish survival without an ethical base is counter-productive and hardly worth the effort. Like the biblical prophets, Jewish dissenters think that Jewish life is only worth continuing if it is faithful to a destiny inclusive of justice and peace. For if, through the transcendence of Holocaust and Israel, Jews join the Other Nations, the Jewish prophetic has to continue on alone. Whether this is possible or not is for others to contemplate. The Jewish prophetic is strictly focused on bringing Jews back to their indigenous prophetic.

Is there a future in the return of Jews to the indigenous prophetic? Rather than retreat, the Jewish prophetic sounds the alarm—there will be no return, there may be no future. The alarm is that everything embodied and struggled for in Jewish history is being squandered. If this continues, the future is mute. As far as the Jewish prophetic is concerned, what reason is there to be Jewish outside the prophetic?

At first glance, the prophetic claim seems self-involved and, as the Jewish establishment continues to proclaim, dangerous as well. True, Jews need some kind of empowerment, as is the case for all minorities across the globe. It may be that Jews need a special level of protection, what with the thousand years and more of anti-Jewish sentiment that continues within parts of global religiosity and culture.

As the Jewish prophetic voice knows well, Israel is helping little in the matter of anti-Semitism and may even be encouraging it to sustain its views about Jews living in a world hostile to Jews. The Jewish establishments sometimes does this, too, as a way of ramping up support for Israel. Thus the accusation that the Jewish prophets, by airing Israel's dirty laundry, are part of the anti-Semitic assault, is dubious. At any rate, the attempt to silence the Jewish prophetic with the danger of anti-Semitism simply heightens the tension.

Though it is difficult to think in these terms today, the Jewish prophetic is on biblical course if it, consciously or unconsciously, encourages Israel's enemies. Remember, in the raw, rather than cleaned up for modern ears, the biblical prophets are scorched earth. At times, God uses Israel's enemies to deal with its intransience. If you want to find what would be popularly considered anti-Semitism today, look no further than the biblical prophets preserved in the Jewish canon. The prophetic condemnation of Israel's behavior and the penalties meted out for them in the Bible make the Jewish prophets of our day seem pale in comparison. This, without forgetting that the biblical prophet's condemnatory message focusing on Israel's sins is, unlike today, sanctioned by God.

With God's sanction, according to the Bible, the prophets throw the exile book at Israel. Which ultimately means the end of everything. If only Israel hadn't lost its way. If only Israel had turned from its wayward path back to God, the way back being justice. In the Bible, the secret is out: Israel isn't coming back. And when some Jews return, the thinking Bible reader knows that the return will likely end badly.

In ancient times, Moses predicted the bad ending in his Deuteronomic lament before the Israelites crossed into the Promised Land. From that moment on, the Promised Land has always been on the cutting edge of unholiness. This is why Israelis of our day,

Our Prophetic Future

who have left Israel and pine for Palestine, are holed up in the Diaspora which they never quite assimilate to. Theirs is a permanent exile because, having re-entered the Promised Land, they know the score first-hand. Fleeing Israel without finding a home among the Other Nations, these Israelis are stuck in a Jewish time warp. The Jewish boots on the ground in Israel, leaving, pining for Palestine, search for a way forward. The quandary is stultifying, the way forward blocked.

Historically, Jews made their peace with the biblical prophets by canonizing them. From that moment on the prophets remain in the textual and liturgical mix, mostly as a corrective to the mainstream life of Judaism as a faith. How could Jews in exile from the land have it any other way? As minorities stretched across the globe, various Jewish communities learned to survive and thrive, often in cultures that were barely hospitable, if at all, to Jews. Diaspora Jewish communities hunkered down, hoping to keep the local religion and culture happy enough to at least tolerate a Jewish presence.

Negotiating a Diaspora Jewish presence came to an end in the Holocaust and in the birth of the state of Israel. A strange thing happened in this ending and new beginning. The tables were turned upside down. Almost annihilated in Europe, Holocaust survivors on the run, Israel, which claimed to represent Jews everywhere, was founded, but on the ethnic cleansing of the Palestinian people.

After the Holocaust emergency was over, Israel continued to expand to the detriment of Palestinians. As Palestine and Palestinian land and life continued to shrink, the basis for the explosion of the prophetic was fashioned. This, even as the prophetic was being driven even further underground due to fears, real or imagined, of a second Holocaust. Without power Jews could hardly afford the prophetic. With power, Jews can't afford the prophetic either.

Performing the prophetic—encountering those on the other side of Jewish history and protesting on behalf of Palestinians in word and deed—is done in solidarity with Jewish history. The prophetic is being performed within and outside Israel, among those Jews who leave Israel and those who have never lived there, including Israeli soldiers who break their silence on what they have done to Palestinians at checkpoints, home invasions, Israeli prisons, and in war. Jews of Conscience do not want racism, colonialism, and apartheid to be Jewish-identified. How can they speak to the world about racism, colonialism and apartheid, as Jews, if Jews are practicing all three?

The mainstream Jewish community is cutting the legs out from under the Jewish prophetic on the global scene by practicing these social, economic, and political evils at home. So the Jewish prophetic has returned home because it understands the stakes involved. When Jews take on injustice as an entitlement, using past suffering as a justification, the final assimilation is at hand. All prophetic hands on deck!

All prophetic hands on deck, that is, when Jewish history is going down. Like the Titanic, so advanced in its day, and how successful we are now, but, without warning, in linear historical time that is, Jewish history is taking on water. Already sunk? It seems that the final battle against assimilation to unjust power is occurring. Is it already over?

It is difficult to imagine how this assimilation can be reversed. Will only fragments of Jewish history survive? If so, which ones? Already there are salvage experts trying to match fragments and glue them together so the next generation can imagine what it was like when Jews fought against oppression.

Perhaps what is salvaged will find the light of day in Jewish museums of the future, museums that locate their collections as "After the Holocaust and After Israel." Will Jewish children of the next generation come to these museums housing prophetic artifacts of what was and understand in a new way their connection to Jewish history? Non-Jews might visit the museum, too, and wonder why the ethical history of Jews ended so suddenly. Like Jews who visit the cemeteries of Germany with Jewish headstones dating back centuries, and then end in 1938, 1939, or 1940, Jews of the next generation might date the end of ethical Jewish history in 1948, 1967, 2017, or 2025. Will Jews in the future wonder why the Jewish ethical landmarks suddenly ended there?

Our Prophetic Future

The Jewish—and non-Jewish—children of the future will make of the museums dedicated to Jewish ethics what they will. No doubt Palestinian children will have their own take on the permanent exhibits as well as special exhibitions that feature the Jewish dissidents of our day. Museum signage will have to instruct the visitors and encourage their exploration into seemingly foreign territory: "You see the concept of ethical Jews, Jews as they were for so long, you remember, the ones who gave the prophetic to the world and embedded the critics of Jewish empire in their texts? If you don't know this kind of Jewishness, those Jews, settle back and let us tell you the story."

PROPHET TRAUMA/PROPHET MYSTICISM

The salvage operation of the shattered Jewish ethical tradition might preserve the memory of what was once the center of being Jewish. Will it also dredge from oblivion the God of the prophets who, at one time, but not lately, was with Jews in good times and bad? Like the Jewish ethical tradition, Israel's God is shattered, in pieces, needs to be located and carefully excavated so the presence of the God That Was will be preserved, at least as an artifact. The kind of artifact that is so out of place, so different, archaic and, yes, weird, that unexpectedly these Jewish—and non-Jewish—children in the future might explore Artifact God as if it could become present again.

The ethics that were, the God That Was, salvaging the remnants. Witnessing to Jewish ethics at the end of Jewish ethical history and the God that fashioned those ethics. Was it all a giant illusion? When history flashes before your eyes and you know that the likes of it won't be seen again, doubt is inevitable. Were Jewish contributions to the world, framed by tremendous suffering, worth it?

Jews think they inherit their history whole. With this acquired knowledge, will they think it wasn't real, meaning that their Jewish inheritance is a fraud? Going into mourning is hardly a way forward but, in reality, dissenting Jews are already there.

No amount of mourning is going to bring God back into being. For the Jewish prophetic every attempt to conjure God has failed. The rabbis lament for the God That Was is more authentic than the incantations of progressive and renewal Jews who, truth be told, borrow, or expropriate, any and all spiritualities to make God real. Quite a task to make the Jewish God of Liberation reappear.

Be careful what you wish for in God's reappearance, though. God rarely reappears the way we want God to anyway, since God's purported reappearance in various Jewish communities has worked to blunt the force of the naked and unadorned Jewish prophetic. For prophetic Jews these are rear-guard actions which only delay the reckoning. The God That Was isn't returning.

Prophetic Jews are witnessing Jewish history at its end. They don't have the power to change the course of Jewish history and, though the jury is still out, since history itself may intervene in ways we do not know, the handwriting on the wall is unmistakable. The Jewish prophetic may be part of a last-minute intervention, perhaps on the margins, since the prophetic center rarely holds. If the prophetic center does not hold, what does?

If meaning and God are past and the Jewish ethical tradition is a memory only, the religious configuration of Holocaust and Israel continues only because of Israel's power over others. How, then, do the Jewish prophets keep arriving, with so much energy? Like a car running on empty, it seems only a matter of time before the prophetic shuts down. But the Jewish prophets seem unaware or perhaps uninterested in the slim pickings of the future.

Subconsciously at least, dissenting Jews must think that the Jewish future will take care of itself, if only they are faithful. Within the collapse, the most obvious question then is—Faithful to what? To which the most concise response from the Jewish prophets is— "Not in Our Name." Details beyond this proclamation, though, are hard to find. It seems that the question to the Jewish prophets is asked and answered. Too simple, perhaps. Yet the shortened prophetic responses are a tradition itself.

Our Prophetic Future

Once called, the biblical prophets can be endless and eloquent in their locutions. They use almost every metaphor in the book, so asked and answered doesn't apply for them. One wonders if the layers of the prophetic have become internalized over time. This may account for the lack of speculation and questioning today on the question of God. As the outer shell of Jewish life collapses, the inner core of resistance becomes stronger.

As the prophetic explodes within the collapse of Jewish life, we may have entered an era of prophetic mysticism. Since even the esoteric, let alone obvious traces of the mystical, are absent in the increasingly naked and unadorned prophetic, perhaps invoking the mystical in relation to the prophetic is akin to praying for miracles. Like the Catholic Church does when they are in search of sainthood?

Mystical credentials may be important yet the Jewish prophetic is unlikely to be found on stage asking for volunteers to experience the laying on of hands. Something else is at work. Mystical, strictly speaking, religious, strictly speaking, or secular, strictly speaking, barely addresses this phenomenon. Perhaps the Jewish prophets of our time have had to break through so many religious and secular barriers that, rather than symbolism or creeds, only barriers speak to them, first one, then another, with more to come.

Even the biblical prophetic tradition is a barrier now to the contemporary Jewish prophetic. This because it is so neatly tucked into the Jewish canon and, on occasion, politely invoked only when it stays far from Israel's abuse of power. Though the secular tradition of the Enlightenment seems the Jewish prophetic's natural modern home, this, too, has become a barrier.

Modernity's promise, at least as the industrial powers of the world interpret it, is drowning. What was thought to be rational has turned irrational in light of the earth's imminent ecological collapse. Much like what was thought to be religious has turned out to be irreligious, so the Jewish prophetic is between the religious rock and the secular hard place, seemingly stranded, without being conscious or articulate about the conundrum. Providing the possibility of a new bridge over the world's terribly troubled waters?

If our Jewish waters are troubled, profoundly so, and it is doubtful they will get better, why mess about with Jewish identity and particularity? When confronted with the global catastrophe, turning inward seems counter-intuitive, retro, and possibly contributing to the problems we already have with group identity, religious and otherwise. Bothering with the questions of Jewish identity and particularity may be seen as a recipe for backsliding into who is what and who isn't, like the old religious quarrels returning for another round of bloodshed.

The Jewish prophetic is on board with these understandings and, without conscious attention, has done away with these seemingly retrogressive barriers. Yet, curiously, the Jewish prophetic has done so in a most peculiar way. Prophetic Jews, having railed against the tired and destructive identities of every group identity formation under the sun, including their own Jewish identity, have further distanced themselves from their Jewish identity and mainstream Jewish identity, curiously by reengaging their identity - by reengaging as Jews. In order to destroy it once and for all or by destroying Jewish identity as it is today and actually save it?

As Jewish history enters a terminal phase, the lesson may be that "terminal" is a state of mind. For the Jewish prophets, terminal as a state of mind reengages "Jewish" by deconstructing injustice perpetrated by Jews. Here mourning and despair, always joined, are transformed into energy to generate heat and light, itself a hope for the future. This kind of hope is embodied in the prophetic itself. For the prophetic carries the collapse of ethical Jewish life and a Jewish future embracing ethical life beyond the collapse in its very witness.

A Jewish future beyond the collapse is without a roadmap, since a roadmap is most useful when continuity is at stake. In the present state of collapse, the future cannot be borne by developing a chart or a mission statement with targets and achievable goals. Instead, the Jewish prophetic is a radical decision in the world, a decision that the Jewish community is unable to make, but one

Our Prophetic Future

that, when presented, is a stark reminder that Jewish life is a reality existing in the world regardless of what Jews today do or don't do. In fact, the reality of "Jewish" becomes more starkly alive in its very abuse. For the abuse of Israel's destiny as a people only points to the final reckoning involved. That reckoning isn't going anywhere except into a deeper exile where the prophetic lives and breathes.

Deep in exile, without hope of return, the prophetic, Jewish and otherwise, breathes deep and free. Over time boundaries and burdens of the prophetic shift, are thought of differently, come to the fore and recede. The trauma of exile, the trauma of the prophetic, remain, but, as well, change shape. As the prophet breathes free, she breathes deeply, feels alive even with age and perhaps more with age since the illusion of victory and defeat are transposed into an embodied fidelity survived through the years.

The prophet has lived the thread his inheritance bequeathed to him and walked a fine line. When fallen, from great heights or sinking deeper into the abyss, the prophet rights herself. The legs of the prophet, already strong, grow stronger over the years. For there is no one who can be faithful for the prophet, though her fidelity is dependent on others as well. Carrying the memory of what was as a future is, in the end, a joint enterprise, with individual legs, churning with others against the tide.

The prophet is alone, most of the time. The prophet is with others, some of the time. Even with others of like mind, though, the prophet knows shared time is limited and somehow contrived. When religious ritual is attached, aloneness is magnified. Religious legitimacy does little to deflect the trauma of the prophetic or transform it. Well into the often sung, "We Shall Overcome," the prophet knows overcoming is unlikely. Everyone in the prayer circle must know this at some level, the prophet surmises.

Has religion become just this, even in its prophetic mode, a faux overcoming because the truth about our fidelity is too difficult to reckon with? The fidelity of the prophet is to be embraced without a sense of accomplishment or elevation now or in that ever-elusive hereafter. Songs with hands held, prayers with heads bowed, the dream that is lifted up, have their place in the prophetic journey. Still, the prophet makes a huge mistake if she thinks of these moments as anything more than a brief respite from an eyes wide-open, alone journey, until the end.

And the times the prophet is not alone, when solidarity eclipses solitude or when a another person enters the stage who the prophet loves and, in turn, is loved by, what then? The prophetic recedes for those moments or, in another way, is fulfilled. Remembering that the prophet's marriage—to the prophetic—is made in heaven. Or is it made here on earth?

Wherever the prophet's marriage is made, it is permanent. No divorce is allowed or, rather, possible. Nor is the way around the marriage, annulment. If the prophetic is embodied it hardly matters how difficult the trauma is or will become. So when love enters into the prophetic equation the prophetic marriage has to be factored in as prior, for a lifetime. Is love with another, for the prophet, like taking a second wife or husband?

The prophetic trail is full of prophets who went before and those living today. Love would do those walking their last mile through thick and thin a world of good, that is if it doesn't divert them from their destination. Can the prophet's aloneness and suffering lead to redemption? The power of love, universal or intimate, leaves the world for others unchanged, but what if it changed the world of the individual prophet? Though individual, this would be better than nothing.

Are Buddha's bones to be discovered on a hillside, as some speculate? Are they resurrected, as others wonder? Like Ezekiel's dry bones, dead on arrival, then breathed into a new existence? Like Pentecost fire or Moses' Sinai tablets being flung to the ground, shattered, then reappearing, the Law resurrected?

Perhaps God has been flailing about, trying to get it right, then knowing it isn't going to be.

The Promised Land became a disaster pretty much right away. Thus the biblical prophets, but they don't go there, not to the ethnic cleansing origins of Israel's entry into land. Or rather the biblical prophets go back beyond the Exodus and somehow skip the ethnic cleansing. Is that what dissenting Israelis are on about,

Our Prophetic Future

going back in history to correct the original promise, turned disaster, with conscience?

The prophets rummage through Jewish history. Jewish empowerment is accomplished, finally and once and for all, and these Jews have the audacity to rock the Jewish boat. How dare they! Do they want Jews to be as pure as snow, perhaps fall back into the pre-Holocaust condition, somewhat like the Third World Other Nations? Or perhaps Jews going the way of Argentina, mid-level, rather than the whole way down. Thus the abyss as defined by those in power.

The dilemma for Jews is real after all. If empire protection of Jews in Israel and America vanishes what will happen to Jews? After all these years, Jewish empowerment is still totally dependent on the Other Nations or at least some, Europe and especially America. An interdependent empowerment is still a long way off. Do the Jewish prophets care about Jews slip-sliding into the Two-Thirds World? With their critique of Western imperialism and American and Israel power it might seem they're hardly paying attention. Should they?

In the final years of any conquest, Israel included, the legions of true believers thin. The will to victory, so strong at the beginning, with an unquestioned ideology and a pretense to innocence so real you can taste it, wanes as the casualties mount and the criticism of organized destruction proliferates. Israel's occupation of Palestinian land can be marked from 1948, the creation of the state, or 1967, with Israel's victory, its permanent expansion into Jerusalem and the West Bank.

Either way, the time frame is long and permanent. Both landmark events mark a definitive turning point in Jewish history. Rummaging through Israel's history, the ethnic cleansing of Palestine becomes a book, written by an Israeli historian, *The Ethnic Cleansing of Palestine*, which sums up the dilemma Jews face. What do Jews do when Jewish redemption is a catastrophe for the Palestinian Other? Should we record our conquest in a biblical book, say the Book of Palestine, and read it in synagogue as a counter-narrative to our sense of innocence and redemption?

Finding Our Voice

As with any group, there are some Israelis who will carry out unjust policies without qualms until the end. Yet more and more Israelis find a redline they can no longer cross. Once a redline is drawn under a redemptive destiny that causes catastrophe for the Other, defection begins and spreads. That defection is fought on all levels. This includes the banning of the Other's commemoration of their catastrophe, the *Nakba*, when Palestinians were cleansed from what became Israel.

Yet many Palestinians and some Jews see the Palestinian *Nakba* as an ongoing event. Palestinians are still being driven from their land. Instead of the Jewish establishment in Israel and America recognizing the historical and ongoing *Nakba*, the movement of dissent supporting boycotts, divestment and sanctions (BDS), for example, is declared illegal in Israel.

Those who propose BDS in America are hunted down, censored and disciplined. Dissent has to be put down. Dissent grows. A prophetic wildfire ignites and spreads. Though the volunteers on the frontline of injustice dwindle, the power of the Israeli state and the Jewish establishment in America expands and becomes more vicious. Any Jewish dissident worth her salt knows that there is Jewish power around every corner in America. The Palestinians are likewise surrounded by Israeli power. Jewish power knows every breath the Jewish prophets and Palestinians take.

Jews were in Palestine for many, many centuries, and lived mostly peacefully, without a state of their own. Indeed, Jews were more or less everywhere around the world as a self-organized minority in larger, non-Jewish, political configurations. Jews Without Borders? Yes, except for the borders Jews drew and the ones drawn around them by others. Peculiar and, for the most part, unstable borders they were. Nonetheless, Jews survived without a military, without redrawing their neighbor's borders and by refusing to covet their neighbor's feudal enclaves, kingdoms and states. Instead, Jews thought and prayed and invoked Zion, hoping for next year in Jerusalem.

Until next year arrived as this year. When the dream of Zion became a reality it quickly became a nightmare. Or, better, a

Our Prophetic Future

quagmire, with ever-expanding Jewish-only settlements, advanced military weaponry field tested on defenseless Palestinians and political and religious discourses that increasingly resemble the early Nazi years.

Would the present impasse have been avoided if the Holocaust and the birth of the state of Israel had not occurred? That's history's wishing well. The coins tossed in the fountain don't make the Holocaust and Israel disappear. Yet the trajectory Israel has taken, ethnic cleansing, permanent occupation, forever armed to the teeth, with Palestinians and others crushed under the mobilized Star of David, is fated. Since there must be a negotiated other way, why, oh why, does Israel refuse to take what it has, settle its accounts and move on?

Every serious peace plan floated over the last decades has Israel in the driver's seat. Still Israel balks. The reason is obvious: Israel has become drunk on a violent form of Jewish destiny, an apocalyptic state-Jewishness, where Israel takes every last dunam of Palestinian land, no matter the consequence. The thinking of Israel's leaders? If Israel can get through the next decades of occupation, final victory is assured. By then, so they think, the Palestinian question will be silenced once and for all. Why get cold feet now?

Do those children and grandchildren of Holocaust survivors who oppose the oppression of Palestinians have cold feet? Or is their conscious desire to end the Holocaust trauma by working toward justice for Palestinians a way for them to land on their feet with their conscience intact? The Holocaust trauma of the past, coupled with the new trauma of oppressing another people, has proved too much for some. True, most Jews in Israel and around the world thought the only way to end the trauma of the Holocaust was to defend themselves until the Holocaust-like siege was over. Then the expansion of Israel took hold, with war after war that could no longer be justified as self-defense. The Holocaust trauma expanded, too, and was used as a justification for the occupation of Palestinian land and people.

As the decades wore on, Israel's innocence became suspect. Used as a blunt instrument of oppression, the bottom fell out of

Finding Our Voice

Holocaust memory. The process on the Jewish side was short in duration, only decades, but for Palestinians these decades were like the longest of nights. The arc of the Jewish universe hasn't bent toward healing. The arc of the Palestinian universe hasn't bent toward justice.

Prophetic Jews search for a way out of the Holocaust/Occupy Palestine trauma. They seek to bend the arc of the universe toward justice. When the moral arc doesn't bend, the bottom falls further. Now more and more Jews of Conscience, sometimes quite reluctantly, understand that there isn't going to be an end to Israel's aggression. Jews of Conscience realize further that Israel's aggression is now global, with armaments and security services being Israel's cutting edge businesses. Regionally, Israel feasts off dictatorships and even genocidal regimes around the world. So it goes. The Jewish prophetic watches the trauma deepen on all sides, including its own.

Trauma is individual, as we know well. Trauma is also collective, though we rarely think in this way. Usually, trauma isn't either/or, it is both, individual related to a collective trauma. This "both" is true in Jewish history, but obviously in Black and Palestinian history, too. When a community is traumatized and then traumatize another people, using the community's trauma as a blunt instrument against another community, trauma blow-back is inevitable. There are those few who see through the trauma landscape and sort out what is real and what is manufactured, since trauma has many angles. The role of the committed intellectuals and activists who stride the world staring in the face of trauma is to discern the dimensions of trauma and how trauma is used. Add the tradition of the prophets embodied in a post-Holocaust/Israel/Occupy Palestine Jewish world, with the desire for light instead of spreading darkness without end. The conditions are ripe for the explosion of the prophetic.

Our Prophetic Future

PROPHET CONFESSION

The prophetic explosion against the Jewish abuse of power had to come. This is why the pressure against dissent is applied directly and without mercy. Instead of using the Holocaust as a bridge of solidarity to others who are suffering, Holocaust memory is a battering ram to silence Jews and anyone else who finds their voice, a voice that should have spoken out and been heard from the beginning of the Palestinian catastrophe and, with few exceptions, was silent.

The reality of the Holocaust and then its misuse drowned out the cries of those who had nothing to do with the Holocaust and wanted nothing to do with Israel as a Jewish state. Why would Palestinians want anything to do with an Israel that causes so much suffering, this in the name of (past) Jewish suffering?

So the charge of anti-Semitism against Palestinians was bogus from the beginning. Palestinians wanted the land they were thrown out of. Wouldn't you? Still, the charge grew leaps and bounds until a rational discussion of the situation of Jews and Palestinians was almost impossible to have, at least in Europe and America. It is happening today, though, led by Palestinians and prophetic Jews who know and embody this unfolding trauma and history by heart. Found here is another and expanding definition of the Jewish prophetic as embodying the unfolding trauma and history of Jews and others, especially Palestinians. Emphasizing the three parts, unfolding, trauma, and history, since the prophetic isn't static or a noun.

The prophet and the prophetic are always on the move. They embody the unfolding trauma and history before them as a delicate and coarse entity which, because the prophet is against the tide, causes more confrontation and, yet with a cautious realism, is the only hope available. For if the prophetic goes pie in the sky, it becomes a religious liturgy best performed in the cathedrals of our world, including our plush synagogues where the elite of Jerusalem and Washington gather for prayers. This is true especially on Yom Kippur, the Jewish day of atonement, which the Jewish community observes without making the central confession of the wrong being done to the Palestinian people.

Is the Jewish prophetic that confession, embodied? Yes, the prophet is more than pleas for justice. The justice the prophet seeks is much deeper than justice as we usually think of it. The prophet is about the possibility of meaning in our lives and history. At this level, the prophet moves deeper, into mourning, then to confession.

Confession is fundamental to turning away from the wrong path and toward the right one. Biblically defined, the prophet is about the demand and hope of turning toward the good and away from evil. Yet we now know that even our scorched earth biblical prophets—those fire-breathing condemners of Israel, those hope-no-hope prophets who re-imagined Jewish life after devastations—were too optimistic. Innocent? Which is amazing, since the biblical prophets were viewing Israel's depravity through the eyes of God. Did God, who knew it all, romanticize Israel?

In the Bible, God knows the score, and notifies the prophets of that fact, even when commissioning them. This is quite startling when you think about it. God sends a messenger with a message that God knows is already doomed and, equally startling, lets the prophet know how the scenario will unfold. Instead of allowing the prophet's innocence to wear off gradually, even as a strategy.

God throws the prophets into Israel's fire with hardly a second to breathe hope. What kind of God is this? Does this God love the prophets? Today there is no God and no innocence. How deep, then, is the love of the Jewish prophets who venture into harm's way without the prospect of Israel turning?

Trauma, history, unfolding, the prophetic is always *en route* to the next question. The prophet embodies the next question, which is what makes the prophet and the prophetic so disturbing. Who wants the next question when the previous question is still fresh and unanswered?

The powerful in politics and religion constantly attempt to keep the next question from being asked. Thus the orthodoxy of the powerful, even if they were once the insurgents. It is hard to

Our Prophetic Future

keep the next question door open. And since power demands privacy in its public life, the prophetic always exposes that privacy, in public. In politics, civil religion attempts to keep the lid on. In religion, liturgy attempts to keep the lid on. It is the prophet and the prophetic who ignite the dynamite of the next question which, paradoxically, has already arrived. This, because the present is already here, mingled with the future. The asked and answered question is also *en route* to the next question that has already arrived. For the Next Question Prophets it is simple. Why don't others see the obvious?

The Next Question Prophets are correct, the central issue in Jewish history is the crisis in Israel-Palestine. While the accusation by some non-Jewish activists, that Jews treat Palestine and Palestinians as a Jewish issue, is on the mark, should the Jewish prophetic thus be admonished, shamed as it were, into divesting itself of what remains of Jewish history? Most of the Jewish prophetic is onboard with a deep critique of Israel as a Jewish state. Most are through with Jewish life in all its forms, except, as it turns out, with its indigenous form, the prophetic. Most prophetic Jews for justice certainly talk little about their Jewishness in public. For them, the Jewish identity issue seems silly. As if on the Left, claiming the indigenous prophetic would seem to be invoking, yes, once again, Jewish privilege.

Just because dissenting Jews rarely announce Jewish privilege hardly means it doesn't exist. Jews are entitled to their special witness, aren't they? Why not let one's Jewish light shine? As if the people around these Jews, Jewish and non-Jewish alike, don't notice the shining light is Jewish anyway. Jewish light is the same light as non-Jews shine, to a great extent. And, yes, to make a big thing out of Jewishness is hardly politically correct or Jewishly correct either.

Yet, as Jews have noticed throughout history, for better and worse, others let their particular light shine and sometimes Jews are part of a larger group, say Woman Light Shining. The Jewish prophetic notices Black Light Shining, Latino Light Shining and often finds the Other Nations' Light so fascinating, wonderful, full of life, even enthralling and seductive. Could it be that the Jewish prophetic's recognition and solidarity with Other Nation's Light deepens as Jews embody their indigenous Jewish Light?

The Jewish prophetic doesn't want the Other Nation's Light hidden under a bushel of universalisms. No way! A world deprived of their particular light would be half as interesting or alive if their light became one light. Notice, too, that even as Jewish dissenters sing the praise of universal light they know it won't happen in their lifetime. Where would prophetic Jews be singing then, in a universal choir, in white robes, under the sign of the Cross? Or in an Ancient Wisdom/New Age worship place where the gathered congregation jump through fiery tubes, hear a Buddhist bell gong and watch the crystals guide them as they walk along Labyrinth Road? Prophetic Jews want diversity raw, uncut, so they can whirl into a broader community that frees them from the Jewish chains that bind. Is the Other Nations' light any freer than the Jewish light some Jews hide?

To be honest, though, the ambivalence about Jewish Light is everywhere, even among the prophetic communities around the world. Prophetic Light is now thought of as humanity's light without being beholden to any tradition or community. So when the origins of the prophetic in the Bible are noted, they are usually classified as biblical in a general way. When, on occasion, the specific Jewish origins are stated, it is considered a historical reference rather than a present day attribution. Yet isn't it strange that when the prophetic is hinted at or announced as ancient or in general, Jews are standing right there as the statement is read? Perhaps this is how Native Americans feel standing right in front of us when America's founding is celebrated, as if their presence is historical only, expropriated and consumed by others.

For a Jew, it isn't happenstance, a delightful coincidence, that the prophetic is alive in us. Especially with all the wonder and misfortune that attends the prophetic. The prophetic is a (mis)adventure too significant to land randomly at any address. It is less about Jews being better or different. The difference Jews acknowledge and welcome in others, let's face it, the difference in

Our Prophetic Future

others Jews sometimes seek, behold and need, is a difference deep inside of Jews, too. Does it need to be said: "Jewish prophets of our day, behold your own difference. Share that difference with others. Be grateful!"

The Jewish prophetic shines bright, like other prophetic light. These lights come from the dark corridors of particular histories. Jewish Light comes from far away, within history, it is ancient light, refracted, with twists and turns, coming from here and there, and Somewhere Else. Perhaps the prophets of all nations come from Somewhere Else. The prophetic is like a mansion with many rooms, a room for the prophets of every nation. In suites with connecting rooms? Hotel Prophets, reserved in advance for?

Even if the prophets from all nations share suites, each room is bound to have its own decor. It stands ready for the arrival of the individual prophet. Custom decorations? Do the prophets have their say or are room decorations prefab, laid out in the way that history dictates? After all, even the prophets from the same nation have their individuality.

So imagine the decorated rooms of African American prophets. With the likenesses of Martin Luther King Jr. and Malcolm X, Harriet Tubman and Sojourner Truth. Prophet rooms from Latin America might include portraits of Gustavo Gutierrez, Leonardo Boff, Elsa Tamez, and Ivone Gebara. For the rooms of the Jewish prophets, featured Jewish iconic figures might be Martin Buber, Abraham Joshua Heschel and Hannah Arendt. It is difficult to imagine images of Jewish icons only, though. As likely, images of Mahatma Gandhi and Oscar Romero would be found. Dorothy Day and Daniel Berrigan?

Strange how often the Jewish prophets look outward for sustenance while others build on the Jewish prophetic without mentioning Jews. A sore point is how many non-Jews use the Jewish prophetic for their own prophetic vocation but rarely link with the prophetic Jews who are joined to their hip protesting against injustice. Though often unintentional, the connection is an obvious one to make. Certainly if you are talking about Native and African

Americans, the connection between history and the present is a no-brainer.

Often the physical appearance of the minority makes the linkage. For the most part, Jews in America are white and many Israeli public intellectuals featured on the world stage have European and American backgrounds. Therefore the Jewishness they submerge is easy to converge with others as well. Add the ambivalence about the state of Israel and Jewish power in America, along with ambivalence about Jews in general, it might be a cunning strategy among Jews and non-Jews to play down the Jewishness of the prophetic Jews involved.

Some progressives take issue with the number of Jews involved in social justice movements, the high percentage of Jews in leadership positions within activist organizations and the outsized contributions of Jews in intellectual circles. Calling attention to prophetic Jews even in positive ways highlights the high percentage of Jews on the opposite, empire, side as well. Prominent Empire Jews are either highlighted as Jews or their identification as Jews is purposely downplayed, lest "Jews-rule-the world" conspiracy theorists take a significant role in progressive movements. Of course, all of this attempt to repress "Jewish" simply points out what the Jewish and non-Jewish prophetic knows only too well: that Jews are major players on both sides of the Empire Divide.

Jews disguised. How visible Jews become when Jews on both sides of the Empire Divide exist as the only folks without having their identity named. An Empire Jew is white. So, too, a prophetic Jew. The Jewish business woman who crashes another glass ceiling is white. The Jewish feminist on the barricades for women's rights is white. One of the most highly regarded intellectuals in the world, Noam Chomsky, is white.

Does it matter that Chomsky's first name is Avram, that he was raised in a Jewish home and that he can only be partially understood outside his Jewishness? Affirming Chomsky as a Jewish intellectual raises the question of where his intelligence leads, at least for some. Chomsky is too clever by half. Is he part of a Jewish

Our Prophetic Future

scheme, twisted as usual, to "dominate" radical politics as Jewish business people "dominate" the economic system?

Imagine Edward Said being discussed without his Palestinian identity being brought to the fore. In real life, Said, like Chomsky on the Jewish side, wanted to avoid having his thought defined as Palestinian. As if so defined his thoughts on Palestine would be relegated, and therefore diminished, as coming from his background instead of his reasoned intellect. Yet it was and is obvious to everyone, or should be, that both Chomsky and Said would be very different thinkers if they had emerged from a WASP background. How much more interesting and understandable Chomsky and Said are when their particularities are affirmed. That they see the broader world from their particularities is obvious. Shouldn't it also be celebrated?

Are Prophetic Jews reacting against the core culture of modernity that Empire Jews are assimilating to with gusto? Perhaps the world is becoming a mirror image of the Jewish Empire Divide. Jews are on both sides of the Empire Divide but so is every nation, religion and community. In this global struggle adding Jewish to your description might seem like a waste of precious time. With all hands on deck, identity politics is forbidden, being a diversion and what this one and that one thinks of Jews is irrelevant. What side you are on is all that matters when the Sisyphean boulder is being rolled up the mountain and global survival is on the line.

Needed are strong bodies and minds and if Jews can be leaders in one or the other why push the Jewish Question with others? Simple as that, it seems, but then periodically talk about Jews has to be addressed anyway. Have you noticed the issue of Jews often comes up even when almost everyone agrees it shouldn't?

A special strategy has to be hammered out, the most common being that everyone is against anti-Semitism—as a form of racism. Perhaps for some anti-Semitism is summed up as a form of racism. Yet if anti-Semitism is a form of racism it is a long standing one, with distinctives involving religion, culture and politics that have lasted for thousands of years where Jews are present and where no Jew has ever been seen. If prophetic Jews are invisible and visible at the same time, because Jews are in the air, for good and bad, everywhere, there may be little to be done except accept the Jewish fate of being wanted and unwanted at the same time.

THE ENTANGLED PROPHETIC

Periodically, some religious leaders start a campaign to liberate Jerusalem, or the holy parts of it relating to Islam, from Israel and Zionism. Jews? The differentiation between Israel, Zionism and Jews is well put, slicing and dicing what has been recently joined. Can these pieces be torn asunder? Should they be?

The idea that Judaism or Jewishness has been hijacked by Zionism and the state of Israel has a ring of truth. It is convenient, and too easy. As if "Jewish" has ever been, only, individual and Diaspora. In its long history, Jewish has and hasn't been individual and Diaspora. Jewishness today is individual and Diaspora—and more. Zionism and Israel are part of the Jewish material fabric today as they have been in symbolic ways in previous millennia. True, in its founding and subsequent expansion, Israel has gone awry. Does that mean "Jewish" is, has to be, or can be separated from Zionism and Israel? Just because the Holy Land is far from holy for Jews, with injustice and empire running rampant, doesn't mean that history can be disentangled. Rather, Jewish responsibility is highlighted. Should the Holy Land, holy for Muslims or Christians, be separated from Christianity and Islam because when either has power injustice and empire runs rampant, too?

Even now the fantasies of liberating the Holy Land prevail, as if Palestinians would survive their purported liberation. What Palestinians need is real life, ordinary life, a justice that can bring what apocalyptic religious fantasies cannot. Religious leaders aside, the Jewish prophetic has torn asunder Zionism and Israel too easily. They, too, see the apocalypse coming, not in the form of liberating the holy shrines but in the Jewish assimilation to injustice. Nonetheless, whether Zionism and Israel hijacked the Jewish world or not, Jewish is entangled with both. As it has always been in one way or another. The issue is less about untangling what cannot be

Our Prophetic Future

untangled. What Jews and Palestinians need is a movement for justice within their entanglements.

Entanglements are difficult, separated conceptually they stand apart. Entanglements are the spice of life, realities within and beyond us as individuals. Would that we could be purified, released from our past, able to fast forward into a blissful future! Daydreams they are and worthy of contemplation, but they are also unreal, like the search for utopia in the Holy Land. Paradoxically, these very same frustrating entanglements give Israel-Palestine, and Jerusalem in particular, its multi-layered beauty. Encased in violence and occupation now, as it is often been, this is part of the land's history.

That Israel-Palestine needs justice is obvious but, at least for now, it is difficult to envision. Yet even if some justice comes soon, entanglements will remain, many of them less than holy. Some of these entanglements are archaic and absurd and, in turn, ridiculous and delightful. Even the Messiah, past or future, will find it impossible to untangle the Holy Land's mosaic.

The Entangled Prophetic. The prophetic is far from pure. If you wander too far into the weeds of the prophetic, the prophetic enterprise teeters on the brink of collapse. Like the empires it calls out, the prophetic wants justice too much, punishes too decisively and often walks the tightrope of scorched earth and compassion without enough care. Sure, one can tidy up the prophetic as a mouthpiece for what we earnestly desire. Doing that, however, mimics empire's sense of innocence. The real battle between the prophetic and empire is less a black and white dichotomy and more somewhere in between. Rather than the struggle to free itself of entanglements, it is best to attempt to bend the entangled toward compassionate justice.

Archbishop Oscar Romero, now officially beatified, proclaimed a martyr, murdered by the empire, which too often includes the Catholic Church that now honors him. Speaking of the entanglement of the prophetic, it is here in full view. Including Romero's own development, how he looked away, was encouraged to do so, continued to look away, then could no longer. As he predicted before his death, Romero rose in the history of his own people. Romero's image of resurrection in history was so Jewish and so prophetic. Should the Jewish prophets of our own day anticipate that they, too, will rise in Jewish history? Even if the arc of Jewish history will never again bend toward justice, the Jewish prophets have done, are doing, their part. The Jewish prophets are being murdered in different ways.

Should the Jewish prophets of our time, some of whom looked away, were told to, had every reason to and then could no longer look away, think that one day they, too, will be beatified and honored as martyrs? Honors do come the way of some Jews who stand for a limited justice that turns out to be another form of enablement of injustice toward Palestinians. Note here the honors bestowed on Rabbis for Human Rights, an interesting group of rabbis to be sure, but looked at more carefully the organization is suspect. Too often Rabbis for Human Rights functions as a cover for the ever-expanding Israeli occupation by presenting the good face of Jews to the world for all to admire.

Those who are afraid of going the extra prophetic mile, especially some progressive Christians, are quite happy with rewarding Jews who conform to their need for Jews to be just, even if that justice is limited, because the good image of Jews is belatedly crucial to their own faith. If the demonic Jew doesn't work anymore, substitute the good Jew, which means no further exploration is necessary. After all, what if renewed Christians had to go Jewish prophetic in real time?

Still circling Romero's martyrdom. Does the honor conferred have to do with a high ranking member of a religious hierarchy standing up to power, after undergoing a conversion to the poor? Yes, and perhaps this recurring interest of the Catholic Church, and Protestant denominations as well, is symbolic of a need to officially recognize the Jewish prophetic in our time. Like Romero, the biblical prophets were hunted down by the religious hierarchy of their time and rewarded with a permanent place in Jewish history.

The biblical recognition is amazing, when you think of it, because here, unlike in the Christian and Islamic scriptures,

Our Prophetic Future

you have an entire people being exhorted, disciplined and often condemned by the prophets in the most vile language, traumatic visions and concrete punishments. Afterward, the prophets and their critique of Israel are enshrined in scripture, it seems as a permanent reminder. A permanent haunting and forever warning that the destiny God proclaimed for Jews could not be reached without justice. Romero is now elevated. Does this mean that the Christian scripture is expanding to include a critique of Christianity and Christian history?

The fear among some is that Romero's commitment, like the elevation of Martin Luther King Jr. in the American calendar, will be sanitized. Sanitizing is what religions and nations do when they get a hold of a galvanizing figure who, in various ways, they helped murder. This, without admitting their culpability in or even addressing the structures that helped banish the voice they now commemorate. The voice that is still relevant is banished a second time. Sometimes national and church honors are bequeathed posthumously to silence voices that continue to speak to the present and to diminish those voices that are destined to arrive.

What to do with those who bestow the honors which delay the reckoning the honored prophets proclaimed? Is this like enabling Jews who read the prophets out loud and purposefully miss the meaning for Jewish life today? Perhaps silencing through honoring cannot be stopped. Nonetheless, after the honors are bestowed, another wrestling begins to free the prophets from their captivity. The struggle of the prophets in life begins anew in their honored death.

The prophets entangled, canonized, trivialized: their afterlife is different than the life they lived. Resurrected, yes, in a way, and available to be used by the future, true, they are now spoken for. Is their elevation a form of flattery or disdain? A new struggle to claim the prophet, in her name, begins, without a clear victory in sight. But then a clear victory was hardly in sight in the prophet's life either.

Does the prophet, once declared, in whatever tradition, become a form of violence against the prophet himself? Wresting the prophets from assimilation to the powerful in religious and political garb is a consuming enterprise. Is it worth embarking on or is the continuing struggle for justice the only honor worthy of the prophets?

Abundance bequeathed, the lives of the prophets enshrined, we experience what most of us did not witness in person. When you have seen the prophets up close and personal, it is another thing altogether. Like knowing Dorothy Day, Thomas Merton, Rosemary Reuther, Martin Luther King Jr., or Oscar Romero. Up close, we feel the ordinary and extraordinary humanity of the prophet; their cold stare and warm embrace, the prophet sleeping, awaking, tending to and rising above the everyday. The prophet marks time. Until all of a sudden, time is filled with a fierce urgency. The prophet is humanity magnified.

What would it be like to live with Jeremiah, Isaiah, Ezekiel? To have been there when each was commissioned, when they set out on their journey, when they hunkered down, when they were on the run. Think of the times the prophet felt close to God and abandoned by God, the anger they had, the moments when they were overwhelmed and when they were grateful. There, with the prophets of old and those among us, we experience ourselves in another way. The prophetic we witness in others, is this also the prophetic within us?

Do the prophets remain with us because they are canonized by religious and political authority or because they are periodically liberated from their canonized captivity? Like God in religion, the prophets need to be called out, sat down and talked to. We should listen to the prophets with a discerning ear. What are the prophets saying to us? In the texts in which they are preserved, the prophets speak, even when presented to us by those who enable injustice. The prophets resist the assimilation they are offered. One feels for the canonized prophets since the prophetic within us is being assimilated, too.

Our desire to release the prophets from their captivity may represent our hope of being released. Journeying with the captive prophets is also our journey. Though their path was too difficult

Our Prophetic Future

and our path has its own challenges, our journey merges at times. Then the prophetic call within us is liberated for us to respond to. Our call cannot be so different than the ones whom we venerate.

The biblical prophets can't breathe on their own anymore. Even Romero is breathless in El Salvador. Declaring Romero a martyr doesn't breathe life into him in and of itself. The church process, so fraught with a politics foreign to his nature, may diminish some of the strength his image once breathed. The question then: Do we resurrect the prophets by living prophetically? Do we keep the prophets alive by embodying the prophetic in our own lives? If so, we have to learn how to breathe prophetically. For as long as our breathing is prophetic here on earth the prophets who are gone are alive.

The biblical prophets no longer breathe on their own. We have to breathe for them. Others will breathe for the prophets of our day once they cease their breathing. Has any prophet ever breathed on her own? The biblical prophets received their prophetic breath from God. Some desperately wanted to breathe as they had before God called, while others stepped right up. "Send me!" The prophetic voice, too, was received from God: "Say this and that. Then say it again. Don't worry if they don't hear or breathe with you. I have it all in hand. If you get out of breath or lose your voice, don't worry, I'll be there."

So the reluctant and eager prophets are sent into Israel's perilous night. As we read the text we know it isn't going to be a picnic. At first we observe. We watch the prophets feel their way. Then we worry as the emphatic moment gives way to chase. Soon we are hooked on the drama. A deepening crisis looms. The prophet is breathing hard, finding his voice. Soon he is running for his life.

Moving back in the biblical frame, is the prophet leading the charge against empire or has the prophet been set up by God to fail? Like the prophets, Israel is breathing. Israel's breath is hard to follow. Power, yes, the kings are there, as are the priests and the prophets. Let the contest begin. Even when victorious, the prophet breathes loss. We wonder if God is working through the prophet only for show or, instead, if God's power is displayed less to turn the people around than to show them what will happen regardless. The prophets act. The prophet is an onlooker. With the stage set, scenery and location in place, is the dialogue already scripted?

In the biblical script reading between the lines is difficult and intriguing. Deconstructing the prophets and placing them in their time and place is instructive. At the end of the prophetic day, however, with all the silences, redactions, interpretations and canonization, the biblical prophets still breathe fire. The prophets live!

Amazingly, unintentionally, sometimes the liturgical setting resurrects the prophets. The prophets are disciplined, restricted, caged, and taught and yet they retain the ability to catch us up short with their willpower, their fear, and their voice. In turn, their sorrow and mourning overwhelm us. In our day, the martyred Romero knew his end would come like a flash in the night.

Prophetic fear, walking with that fear, is an essential part of the prophetic vocation. Basic prophetic material, like Elijah's queries to God about who will shield and feed him, where will he find shelter and water. The prophets don't live in the sky or walk on water, for the most part, though there's stock rescue miracle footage in the biblical text, too. Editors, then and now, often want to speak for the authors they edit. Nonetheless, the biblical script cannot breathe for the prophets. Just when the prophet's story bogs down, a dramatic breakthrough occurs. We are back on the prophetic journey wondering how the story will end. Even when we already know the ending.

"Our years of winning," Open Hillel, writes. Facebook postings have a way of summing things up too easily. Yes, these Jewish college students are hitting the prophetic path, against the Jewish establishment trying to shut down their dissent on Israel. I doubt most of the students are reading the biblical prophets. They don't need to. Once again, the mysterious persistence of the prophetic. If the established university Hillels ban Jewish speakers supporting divesting from the Israeli occupation of Palestine, you know sooner or later a Jewish revolt will erupt. All the big money in the world, the university connections and charges of anti-Semitism and Jewish self-hate, have little chance against the Jewish prophetic.

Our Prophetic Future

How late this revolt is, with so many Palestinian and Jewish casualties along the way! It takes a while for the Jewish prophetic ball to get rolling. What is Open Hillel winning? Are "we" winning? In demanding the prophetic be heard and by the prophetic voice growing stronger, yes, there is a victory of sorts. Winning as in turning injustice into justice, well, we couldn't be further away. Kudos to those who stand up, and a deserved round of applause. As Israel sinks deeper into the abyss of injustice and Palestinian suffering increases, Open Hillel has found its prophetic voice. Open Hillel is disturbing the empire's script with their youthful hope.

Open Hillel swims against the tide of Jewish history. As well, against the tide of imperial material and military support for Israel from America, Europe and its new Arab strategic base. Yes, as Israel's reputation in the world tanks, its power base in the world grows stronger. Open Hillel can't do much against fighter aircraft from America and nuclear submarines from Germany delivered to Israel. Nor can it make a dent in settlements in the West Bank and armament testing in Israel's multiple invasions of Gaza.

Opening the Israel-Palestine discussion wider is important, but to what effect? Beyond admonishing rhetoric, none of the world's powers are likely to do anything about Israel's abuse of power. So why highlight Jews who find their voice on Israel's oppressive policies and the American Jewish establishment's enabling of Israel? It is all water under the bridge when it comes to Congress and the White House. Not to mention Israel's other great ally, Germany, still in the throes of Holocaust guilt and the fear that homegrown Nazis might make another stab at seizing the initiative.

Open Hillel is too little, too late. Palestine is over in the way it was known and could have been. Every peace process negotiation has been limited; only the relative size of Palestine's destruction is on the table. Israel has never missed an opportunity to expand and close off any negotiation which would limit its expansion. You hardly need to be an anti-Zionist to chart Israel's expansion graph. Every day more land is expropriated and sometimes, especially during war, large land-grabs occur, first-up being Jerusalem, the city where prophets roamed, the Temple stood, and Jesus entered and was led away.

Jesus, as a Jew, experienced the Passion most Jewish prophets experience in one form or another, biblical and now. Without the great Jewish-Christian divide, finalized in the Roman Empire, prophetic Jews and prophetic Christians might recognize this common Passion inheritance. For what is the prophetic without the lash being applied in public? What is the prophet if not crucified in whatever manner is appropriate for the political and religious culture the prophet happens to live within? The Crucified Prophetic. You don't have to be a Christian to know the Passion when you experience it.

Forward into the Christian night? Not even close. Christians who engage the Jewish prophetic, the only place they can go to free themselves of Constantinian Christianity, run straight into Constantinian Judaism when they surface. A contradiction of immense proportions for Christians newly baptized in the Jewish prophetic. Now that they are freeing themselves of their own captivity, prophetic Christians see prophetic Jews freeing themselves. Yes, when they come up for air and see Jews, prophetic Christians think they have found the biblical prophets in modern clothes. They do, though dressed in clothing and with a language that defies any Christian categorization.

Many prophetic Jews hardly know when to bow their heads or how to pray. They have little interest in learning either. The closest these Jewish prophets have come to religion are documentaries viewed in universities depicting various forms of religiosity. On the normative level, most self-respecting Jewish prophets have little to do with the synagogue or any other Jewish institution, the charge being hypocrisy and enablement of injustice.

Yes, times have changed. Empire Jews have gone religious in an empire sort of way. Think of Christians in a cathedral, add plush seating and you more or less get where Constantinian Judaism is. On the Left, there are renewal Jews who wear flashy outfits and multi-colored kippot. Think of the colorful robes some Protestant

Our Prophetic Future

ministers and Catholic priests wear that symbolize the more liberal congregations they serve.

You get the picture. Renewal Jews are serious folks, trying to weave together a progressive Jewishness that prays together. So Jews stay together? Think of them like you think of Christian ministers in jeans strumming guitars. Sure, somewhat of a caricature but it is hard even for Jews to allow the prophetic to remain as it really is. Unadorned, naked, on the run for her life, with whatever ritual once observed dissolved by the corruption of the community.

All communities are corrupt, in the main, if we think of corruption broadly, but whereas some Christians are able to work through the incredible hypocrisy of Christian history and still bow before God, prophetic Jews are ever mindful of the temptations of idolatry. Once there's idolatry in the religious air, Jews are gone, gone, gone, never to return. In Christian terms, think of these prophetic Jews as on their way to Golgotha without any sense of following God and without any foretaste of redemption.

The recounting could go and on but here it is in a nutshell. At the most significant juncture in Jewish history, on the Holocaust/Israel axis, something went horribly wrong. Jews descended into the abyss, on the ground, intellectually and religiously. The civil war fought over the Jewish future between Constantinian Jews and Progressive Jews was false. Both wanted Jewish power to triumph. The difference was the margins. Then Jews of Conscience appeared. In the line of the prophets they were and are harangued from both sides. In the abyss, they think recounting should become an accounting. A reckoning is needed of others which Jews quite rightly demand. Such a reckoning is now demanded of Jews.

A partial reckoning even now delays the reckoning demanded by Palestinians, the world and Jewish history. What did Progressive Jews get wrong? Why have progressive Christians been so timid, including those whose experience in the (un)Holy Land shouts to them of the injustice that Palestinians experience individually and collectively? This experience that Christians, especially from the West, have on the ground, counts heavily. It can serve as a huge corrective against the mostly armchair analysis of

Finding Our Voice

Progressive Jews. Prophetic Jews of Conscience have gone the extra mile now. They know the score. But how to bring this message back to America, where so much power resides and the Jewish community is so tightly interwoven with the kind of power once exercised over Jews?

The reckoning isn't about solutions. Everyone knows what the future holds. Progressive Jews held the line long enough to make sure the future they wanted, minus the placement of the Apartheid Wall here or there, would be assured. You see the basic point of Progressive and Renewal Jews, including Rabbis for Human Rights, is to uphold Jewish innocence in the eyes of others and in the eyes of Jews, too. So the call is to return Jews to their proper place and behavior, as if the Jewish state, without confession and with its history of oppressive behavior, can be Jewish in anything but name only.

This movement, beginning from loss, in the abyss of injustice, is fought tooth and nail. Mourning is difficult. Especially the mourning that resumes life amidst ongoing destruction and death. For the state of Israel, with the help of it enablers, has systematically destroyed Palestine. Is there any other word for it? It is less the religious zealots than the state sponsored aspect of the destruction that should be focused on, with a special eye on the suffering of Palestinians, individually and collectively.

Prophet work it is, biblical style. Since the biblical prophets pointed specifically to how entire classes of people were suffering from dispossession, neglect and exclusion because the social, political and economic systems were so structured. After all, didn't the God of Israel lead the people out of Egypt so that they could construct a new kind of society?

In sociological terms, the Exodus project was defined some years ago as creating a "socially egalitarian, decentralized, tribal democracy," a utopian project that would be quite practical. Like the Jubilee cycle contained in the biblical text, where every seven years, beginning each week with the seventh day, and projecting out to the fiftieth year, society would be leveled and the inequalities of all types accumulated over the weeks, years, and decades, would be put right, back to the beginning, then again after the next accumulation of injustice.

All of this, biblically-speaking, is related to God, who has little interest in sacrifices, incense, or tithing without justice. Interesting, too, that, in various places in the text, this includes everyone in the land, Israelite and stranger, so that the promise of liberation can be heard and practiced throughout the land. The rock bottom experience is that the biblical cycle of justice could be the way to birth a new social order today, in the near future, or decades from now.

JEWISH PROPHETS IN DECIMATED GAZA

The prophet knows catastrophe. The catastrophe doesn't have to be the big one to get the prophet's attention. Suffering, the more the better, engages the world's attention. The more violence the better, too. In our virtual world, with the wealthy on top, photos that tug at our heart strings are best. Thus natural disasters take priority, if natural is the right term, since even earthquakes, at least the damage done, has to do with human preparation or the lack thereof. Wars do well with reporters on the make.

When prophetic Jews went into Gaza in 2014, for example, as Israel's invasion came to a close, they found more than destruction as far as their eyes could see. In the rubble, they found body parts and, as well, the end of Jewish history, its ethical content at least. This, before the testimony of Israeli soldiers on their orders to treat Palestinians who remained alive as life-threatening, therefore a target to be taken out, just like that. Soon Israeli soldiers who served in Gaza and witnessed the destruction Israel had caused—they had caused—broke their silence. In their actions, they, too, witnessed the end of ethical Jewish history.

Why blame the boots on the ground? Israel's High Command sent the soldiers in, Israel's population supported their troops, the Jewish establishment in America had Israel's back. American arms were provided during the war. The criticism of the world powers, even the churches, behind the scenes and sometimes spoken in public, lacked focus and determination. At the end of Jewish history, Jews and others lacked the will to stand up and be counted in an efficacious way. Even threats of evening the score in the International Criminal Court in The Hague seems an eschatological hope delayed in perpetuity. Like the Second Coming of Jesus, it is better to breathe than to hold one's breath.

"Here I am. Send me." To Gaza? Imagine Isaiah in Gaza. The story unfolds. What kind of sending ceremony does Isaiah have so that witnessing a martyred people doesn't scramble his Jewish brain? Walking among the rubble of Gaza, body parts mixed with the debris of modern life, how does Isaiah report back what he witnesses without seeming to be Jewishly self-involved? Since Isaiah sees Jewish history flashing before his eyes, what else can he report?

Flashing forward, years later, almost nothing in Gaza has been rebuilt. Israel has been holding tight on the rebuilding strings—for a profit. Isaiah returns. "Here I am"—at the end? "Send me"—into Gaza's rubble? The scriptures are still being written. Jewish scribes were in Gaza, taking notes, editing and redacting. Secrets are hard to keep. After Gaza, modern day Isaiahs are on the ground. Different Jewish boots. Military. Prophetic. In Gaza as elsewhere, Jews on both sides of the Empire Divide.

Ploughshare Isaiah was eager, biblical GPS switched on, he knows where he stands. Right here. Ready, too. Instruct Isaiah and it will be done. Pronto. So God's instructions to Isaiah—in Gaza? A challenge for sure. Because condemning Israel's invasion is a no-brainer. Consoling Palestinians is a singular challenge. Jeremiah was different. When God called, Jeremiah wasn't ready at all. Or eager. Instead he plead youth and the inability to find the proper words. God had little patience with Jeremiah's excuses. So before Jeremiah knew it, God put words in his mouth.

There was no turning back for Jeremiah and, later, his vast mourning almost overwhelmed him. In light of Jeremiah's fear, God promises to be right there with him, at least at the beginning. Another God promise, if need be God will rescue Jeremiah. So what words would God through Jeremiah have for Palestinians in

Our Prophetic Future

Gaza? In Gaza, who would Jeremiah need to be rescued from, the pummeled Palestinians or the invading Israelis? After all God appointed Jeremiah to be a prophet to all nations. Are Palestinians excluded? Isaiah is right up front. Good for him. Others like Jeremiah, without forgetting Ezekiel, are reluctant. They have difficulty believing what is happening on the ground. Though they are less sure of what will transpire in the future, their initial worry is right-on. Prophet land is fraught. Worse, when some like Amos plead simplicity, a shepherd with nothing much going on upstairs, God isn't buying it. After all, the choice has been made. God will do the necessary work to insure the prophet starts out well-equipped.

Then there's Elijah, the prophet of many lives, including a renewed prophetic calling after botching his initial outings, where he gave it all up, fled, but God doesn't let him go. Soon Elijah is stalked by God and fed by ravens, a nice touch for sure, especially when you worry about where your next meal is coming from. Elijah's prophetic return is important. Tired of Israel's failure to turn around and his failure to turn Israel around, Elijah hangs up his prophetic spikes. The whole enterprise is going down, why bother? Yet God pursues Elijah, asking as he flees: "What are you doing here, Elijah?" Away from the struggle, God instructs Elijah to get up on his feet. There, standing in the open field, Elijah receives new instructions. He returns to the field of battle.

So think of the biblical prophets, updated, with their fiercely honed intelligence, anxiety and reluctance, despair and mourning, now without a God-centered commissioning ceremony, the text remaining to be written. First the prophet is welcomed, then disappears, and unexpectedly is back again. This in Gaza, or the West Bank, or Jerusalem. The prophet witnesses Palestinians in refugee camps throughout the Middle East, travels the Palestinian Diaspora, and soon we are introduced to Max Blumenthal writing of Israel's pervasive racism and hooliganism before it became self-evident in the Gaza war. And on the streets of Tel Aviv, as Jewish thugs harass Jews protesting the bombardment of innocent civilians.

Finding Our Voice

Without warning and without Elijah's chariot, the scene shifts, as it often does in the Bible. We find Blumenthal in Gaza walking through the rubble, collecting experiences of those who survived and then publishing their stories, while tweeting photos of Gaza's Israel-created lunar landscape. Blumenthal, in turn, is loquacious and silent. He writes effortlessly, yet the ease is surface. Blumenthal has difficulty getting to the bottom of what he is experiencing. So he contacts a fellow Jew in the struggle who once strode the hills of Palestine and is now sidelined, waiting for God's call to return to the field of battle. Blumenthal asks what he is experiencing. Echoing Elijah, the veteran Jew of Conscience replies: "Max, stand up. You are witnessing the end of Jewish history as we have known and inherited it."

After Gaza, this last one, but there have many Gaza's, Israeli-style, Jews of Conscience, already on the move, ramped up their efforts, a full-court press, especially Jewish Voice for Peace, whose Haggadot are so provocative. In their renditions of the Passover story, they shift the biblical plagues visited upon the Egyptians to the Ten Plagues of Occupation, Israel is visiting upon Palestinians. Jewish Voice for Peace was on the Gaza invasion from the beginning and their membership soared, so many Jews and non-Jews wanting the madness to end and, yes, wanting the Jewish prophetic to thrive as a witness to Jews, to Palestinians, and to the world.

Even if the abyss is all we have, at least Jews and those in solidarity with Jews and Palestinians could have their voice heard. Inside the Jewish Voice for Peace, a newly formed Rabbinical Council was working overtime. Yes rabbis, a courageous few, well beyond the renewal phase, with some rabbinical students, said the hell with it, it is time to stand up and if we cannot stand up now when would be the time? Like God told Elijah, get back in the arena, victory and defeat is now the skin in the game of fidelity in history as a Jew.

Why be a rabbi if you are unwilling to stand the heat of your own convictions? How long the world waited to hear rabbis chant justice, not liberal side issues which for Jews were easy, but the real

Our Prophetic Future

thing, justice with consequences. So long in coming, yes, but the slaughter of the innocent calls conscience.

Yes, there are failings. Organizing the prophetic troops is important. The missives sent through the internet, however, often lack depth and, too often, Jewish Voice for Peace has difficulty deciding which other justice groups they can engage with without giving everything over to the American and Israeli governments that would only go so far, really not far at all. As in previous administrations, their various peace plans consigned Palestinians to a truncated, ill-defined autonomy, permanently occupied by international troops, themselves, with Palestinians, encircled by Israeli forces. Why sign on to an agreement that seals your fate?

Playing politics is like playing with fire, a dangerous affair for the prophetic, so Jewish Voice for Peace plays it close to the vest. Sometimes they are honest, other times they aren't completely honest with others. With themselves? In the abyss there are few options. The rabbis, too, already out on a limb, are still in the rabbinic mode, Diaspora only for Jews, which, if you think about it, is like trying to return to a place that ceased to exist after the Holocaust and Israel. "There isn't a Diaspora way back," some wanted to say to them, since most Jews are deeply embedded in the American and Israeli empires. It is an unparalleled experience in Jewish history. Diaspora "Jewish" is over. Yet there isn't an (un)Diaspora way forward either. Remnant it is. Prophetic remnant time. Meaning organizing and something more. The "more" hangs in the air, haunting the justice enterprise.

No one can live on the prophetic alone. Without the prophetic all of us are knee deep in complicity. Insurgencies are limited. Insurgents aren't insurgents only, if they have depth. Prophets are unstable, like the God who calls them. The empire wants stability and has its well paid minions. Even the prophets need funds; food is rarely delivered by ravens. In the mix is life, found and lost, with plenty of trauma and mourning, what's lost isn't found and isn't returning.

The center isn't everything, though without a center we are lost. Most of our lives we wander. So, thus, the question of questions: With every proposal inadequate to the task, is it then important to pronounce a solution to situations, including Israel-Palestine, where there are none? And judge others by what they propose, in light of our proposal, neither of which will come to fruition?

Things happen and though the pace of change may, at times, seem glacial, there comes a time when a tipping point is reached. Where little movement was occurring, suddenly there is. Yet even when the tipping point is reached, movement is unpredictable. The steps forward may come in a rush, backward, too. Meaning that change itself, so necessary, is inevitable and fraught. Change demands a steady eye, all hands on deck, but with some remaining a step removed. The prophet, insofar as possible, has to remain, if not outside or above the fray, Somewhere Else.

The criticism is ripe: "Here we are galvanizing and organizing, mobilizing everyone we know and haven't yet met. The prophetic is in motion just like you advocate. All of us know that justice is our marker and anything less be damned. All of us know that we are in the abyss, with everything at stake, our calling, our witness, our destiny. As a people we were called into being to transform ourselves and the world. And there you are, Mr. Prophet, hanging out on the sidelines, monitoring every breath we take? Stalk them, the oppressors, not us!" The letters, thus addressed, sent this way and that, expressing concern and care, anger, too, since it is obvious and hard enough to swim against the tide and fashion a prophetic community out of disaffected stragglers who are heading into exile. Their Jewishness is challenged and derided. And the one who cannot join, except briefly, who also has her own history of derision and more, dwelling so deep in exile, she who is now searching for another name for this experience, for crying out, not in the wilderness, in the abyss that is only beginning to be recognized so many years later.

The prophetic community is looking for an angle, a lever to pry open Jewish history. The justice core, that's what they are looking for. Digging day and night, are we far from finding it? The prophet on the prowl, too, is looking for light. Darkness surrounds

Our Prophetic Future

the prophet but, no matter, light must be around this corner or the next one. The prophet finds fragments of light. Also Jewish power. Yes prophetic light and empire around every corner. So take whatever light is found, embrace it and turn the next corner hoping to find more—light.

Downward mobility has to be factored in. If you haven't yet tasted downward mobility, you are on easy street, with a critique that is manageable for those you associate with and who you think are in your corner. When you begin to slide, however, or go down with a sudden blow, taking a fall, planned by others, orchestrated and paid with millions, then you find out who your friends are or, mostly, were. It is a dog eat dog world for the communitarians among us, too. Risking a livelihood or risking anything, a yearly dinner with the local rabbi for example, it hardly needs to be dramatic. Not at all.

Few are willing to do anything, especially close to home. On the prophetic path, one begins to realize that corruption is deep inside so many of those who are brothers and sisters in arms. Words of support are cheap. The turned back is the rule and should be expected. Yet how sad it is, this part of humanity. Inside all of us. You want to weep and practice self-protection as a martial art, if you can go that self-interested mile and look yourself in the mirror the next morning. Should you pass that on to your children, too, that their father or mother couldn't take it anymore and decided to fold, take their cards and bury their head in the sand until the end?

To what purpose anyway, Palestine is finished, Jewish history is over. The abyss we wallow in is glorified, as if Jewish soldiers defecating in the living room of a Palestinian home they have commandeered is their fate and the inheritance we pass on to our children. In this light, what Christians and Muslims think of Jews is insignificant. Yet, as well, a contributor to their own self-righteousness, the abyss their traditions have traversed and dwell within, too. Is there any option other than cynicism, about the fate of humanity, the earth, and the prophetic?

So the Jewish prophetic has complaints. Yet most prophetic Jews aren't working in the religious terrain and for obvious reasons. After being hit over the head by Christian triumphalism and disciplined by Jewish religious and secular authorities, few prophetic Jews go near a religious institution of any kind, let alone entertain religious discussions. For fear of the rage inside of them, no doubt, and, for them, the obvious silliness of it all. As if there is a God, even of justice. They fail to see such a God operating in the world or can assent to the notion of the "mystery" of God's work, meaning what is not happening in a way that can be seen and documented, is actually happening in a way we can't see, for now, well the Jewish prophetic rightly steers clear of such hocus pocus.

Thus the newly committed rabbis for justice, these rabbis being Jews of Conscience who are working and perhaps even praying for the reversal of the Palestinian catastrophe, they have their work cut out for them. Yet it is far from clear that these Rabbis of Conscience have such an agenda, converting those who have strayed. If you can think "strayed" when secular prophetic Jews are already embodying the Jewish indigenous.

Rabbis of Conscience are out on the limb of Constantinian Judaism, credit where credit is due. Some of them, if not the majority, are playing catch-up, the usual religious thing for all groups. This ought to occasion thought as to why the institutional religious among us are usually behind the justice eight ball and wade into the fray only when they undergo their own conversion to the embodied prophetic. These rabbis are trained in rabbinic texts and liturgy, many in the concept of Jewish civilization, two fascinating and, in the main, outdated understandings of Jewish life. Catch-up is only part of their problem.

As Jewish leaders, according to the seminaries at least, and, as with any rabbi, resting somewhere in their consciousness, Rabbis of Conscience have to reinvent themselves to become who they are called to be. In their congregations and to some extent in the seminaries as well, they have support. They are surrounded, too, with Jews who deride them in their congregations and seminaries. There are outside influences always breathing down the rabbis' necks as well. So their day job hasn't lasted, for some of them, and probably won't last, for most of them, raising the issue of where

Our Prophetic Future

prophetic Jews can meet as Jews, daily or on special occasions, and what is to happen when prophetic Jews meet.

The God question looms, among others. Any attachment to the state of Israel. If Zionism can be broached. If Jews indeed have created and inhabit a civilization, when Jewish history dwells in the abyss, rephrasing Gandhi, when asked about Western civilization, saying it would be a good idea, for Jewish civilization, it would likewise be a good idea, if any civilization can revolve around the indigenous prophetic. The challenge remains. No matter how difficult, there isn't any other place to start than the indigenous prophetic.

A spirituality for the indigenous prophetic? Most prophetic Jews hardly have a place for this on their agenda. True, the prejudice of the religious can run high; to be secular is to miss the meaning of life. Even those religious folks who think they are quite open often ride a high horse. The prejudice of those who abhor religion runs high, too; for many of the secular, to be religious is an intellectual travesty. Somewhere in the middle the twain might meet if the field of battle was cleared of religious fetishisms and secular fetishisms, too.

The divide here is wide. Is there reason to build a bridge over these troubled waters? When the troubled waters of history rise high, each person and community to their own be true. It may be that the embodied prophetic, the indigenous of the people Israel, hardly needs the spirit, however defined, to maintain itself.

Yes, the persistence of the Jewish prophetic has occurred against a backdrop of religious texts or, rather, texts that are known as religious. At first, it seems, the Bible is a recorded history with everything in the world present, including Israel's relationship with God. Everything is connected, life and death, justice and injustice, compassion and violence, God and Gods. If there is a distinguishing moment for what we call religion in the context of a people's life who began by wandering from place to place, then were forced into slavery, soon were on the run, and finally came into the Promised Land.

Finding Our Voice

There are the movable Tablets, Tent of Meeting, priesthood ceremonies, rules and regulations for life and death, boundaries that establish justice, a Sabbatical cycle that redresses accumulated injustice and without forgetting the various Temples where the priests held court. The Bible is a panoply, a fantastic tapestry, without need of romanticizing the earthiness that, relentlessly, too often divides the material world into good and evil. Included is the railing against the Gods that keep popping up and finding their home under every green tree. Jewish history is full of life.

The priests of Yahweh bowing to the sun, Ezekiel's remarkable condemnation that preserved part of the diverse beauty of Israel's struggling tribal confederacy in the land. The embodied prophetic, Israel's indigenous, against the backdrop of what became Judaism, today is deprived. The collapse over the centuries and certainly now has poisoned the religious backdrop, rendered it barely accessible and thus even Judaism's rescue efforts seem forced.

The Jewish prophetic has little need for a religiosity that is part and parcel of the American and Israeli empire landscape and which seeks to make the Jewish prophetic more benign, mainstream, and well-behaved. As if wealthy synagogues on empire's Main Street will discipline the prophetic forever. The Jewish prophetic isn't about to play its part as pillars of the community. Not a chance. So, if the Jewish prophetic needs a backdrop other than the one who may, with others, face trial at at the International Criminal Court in The Hague, the task of making a spirituality for the Jewish indigenous prophetic exist is daunting.

The prophet as an anachronism. An anarchist. The prophet is an analyst of wonder and oppression. The prophet breaks down assumptions that parade as givens. This, with an eye out for widows, orphans, strangers, and the poor. So it was with the cosmic explorer, Albert Einstein, who thought the Jewish massacre of Palestinians at Deir Yassin in 1948 was a stain on Jewish history, and so sought to remap our conception of the universe of mourning the dispossessed and the murdered. Nationalism wasn't going to solve the Jewish Question, Einstein opined. It would only bring it up a notch.

Our Prophetic Future

So Einstein knew from the beginning the level Jews would descend to, under certain conditions. For Einstein, the condition was a state. Yet Einstein did see a need. Jews had been maligned for so long, self-confidence was needed. Especially, as Hitler's shadow spread across Europe. Einstein sought the universal as a way of dealing with the particular he knew always had the propensity to descend into madness. Einstein's view of the cosmic universe was wholly dependent on coming from the Jewish side of the tracks.

Rewilding is not for the faint of heart. Rewilding is the prophetic wild card played when it matters, on its own time. If the prophetic is timeless, most interpretations of the Bible go there, they are a fantastic devotional read and then get on with the rest of your day. The prophetic in time is much more challenging, less devotional or not at all. Yet the timely prophetic is too easily consumed by the battles of the day that have their place on the continuum and ending there until the next battle on the continuum. Continuum leading, where?

Prophetic Red Cards are mostly symbolic now. Though they still carry a force which resounds through history. Like Romero's statement: "I would like to make a special appeal to the men of the army, and specifically to the ranks of the National Guard, the police and the military. Brothers, you come from our own people. You are killing your own brother peasants when any human order to kill must be subordinate to the law of God which says, 'Thou shalt not kill.' No soldier is obliged to obey an order contrary to the law of God. No one has to obey an immoral law. It is high time you recovered your consciences and obeyed your consciences rather than a sinful order. The church, the defender of the rights of God, of the law of God, of human dignity, of the person, cannot remain silent before such an abomination. We want the government to face the fact that reforms are valueless if they are to be carried out at the cost of so much blood. In the name of God, in the name of this suffering people whose cries rise to heaven more loudly each day, I implore you, I beg you, I order you in the name of God: Stop the repression!"

Finding Our Voice

The biblical prophets come alive. From a center of power, humbled and weak. From a man trained in the center of power to maintain that power and represent it. Instead, Romero went rogue. Uttering and proclaiming words that bullets stopped, for a moment. Words that live on. Did Romero think that his words would actually stop the slaughter? Or did he know that the violence against him would only increase and still had to say them, emphatically, so even God could hear them? In his telling, did Romero feel that God filled his mouth with those words, like God's promise to Jeremiah? Even though Romero knew that he was writing a truth that went far beyond him and his time.

Elucidation though abundance and deprivation. Quite a duo. Are they joined at the hip of transcendence and immanence? Are these latter two also joined at the hip of God and justice, God and compassion, justice and compassion? With or without God, or how God has been envisioned? Mostly by those who have not experienced abundance and deprivation? You see the empire types that usually define the terms spiritualize what is hard to quantify. They put into words what can be sung without offending the piety of the faithful. Do the faithful long to experience something that is wrapped up in an inspiring doxology that only theologians can parse?

Epilogue

No matter how many times I try to define the prophetic, I come up short. Too often, I talk and write around the prophetic. Perhaps I am afraid that by defining the prophetic, I might enter into that prohibited realm of idolatry.

Broadly defined, idolatry is assigning a reality to a presence that cannot be objectified. This usually refers to an incorrect understanding of God. In an age where God is more and more difficult to affirm, defining the prophetic should be left open. After all, the prophetic proposes only the possibility of God in the world.

Still, we seek guidelines for the prophetic, what is the prophetic way, and what departs from it. Without such guidelines it is difficult to find our voice.

Perhaps I have failed in my meditations to offer such guidelines. Surely there are other viewpoints, other voices, that can help us draw near to the prophetic.

When my Jewish theology of liberation was published in Spanish for the second time a few years ago, with a new translation and commentaries from well-known Jewish and Christian thinkers, my oldest son, Aaron, was asked by the editor to comment as well. When I learned of Aaron's invitation, I wondered if he could help me with my limitation.

At first I was reluctant to read Aaron's commentary, an understandable anxiety of a father who experiences his son's words as if they are his own. Prompted a second time by the translator, I read Aaron's text. Aaron's words always reflect a justice-oriented compassion. One of the great gifts in my life has been to watch and marvel at Aaron finding his voice.

Aaron's appreciation of what I had given him as a father was pleasing. Yet I knew immediately that he was describing something more. Indeed, Aaron put into words what we both had been given by our tradition: "Indeed, I have inherited an interpretive framework and existential directedness, a way of life toward which to strive. I have been given tools with which I may now seek an intentional orientation toward myself; toward various communities, my own included; toward others; toward the Other; toward the divine; toward the world."

There it is, I thought, the prophetic defined, and how wonderfully wrought, eloquently fashioned, with deep thought, evoking a magnificent image of strength and humility, and right to the point. My second thought: "Typically Aaron."

I began to use Aaron's words to frame my own. Clearly, Aaron, in writing of his inheritance, was speaking for me. I felt an urgency to understand more than his eloquence. I needed to understand Aaron so as to understand myself better. I felt his words pointed to something I had yet to see or, during the ups and downs of life, had buried and forgotten.

So I began to break Aaron's text down, isolating the textual nuances and details for their meaning. For if Aaron, through me, was defining what the prophetic is, he could also help me understand my life and voice in its broader arc. In so doing, he might help others understand their life and voice, too.

I noticed, for example, where Aaron placed the divine in his text. The divine isn't at the beginning or at the end of Aaron's attributes of the prophetic. So situated, "divine" is mentioned once and without capitalization. God is present, God isn't the center. The "other," though, is mentioned twice, once in the plural, once in the singular. Unlike the divine, Aaron capitalizes one of his others. As if the Other is God?

Epilogue

Aaron's "interpretive framework" is compelling. For Aaron, it seems that the prophetic is the lens through which to view himself, his community, and the broader community. Such a framework is critical and compassionate. Above all, it is intentional.

This is where I initially missed part of Aaron's prophetic vision. Re-reading Aaron's text slowly, I noticed a key word I initially misquoted in some of my presentations. Writing Aaron's words down on a hotel envelope right before I spoke at a conference in Houston, I even miswrote the word. In a subsequent conversation, Aaron admonished me: "The word is 'directedness,' Dad," he told me one night on the phone. I had miswrote and misspoke it as "directness."

Directedness rather than direct, signifying/having/being, as Aaron defined it, an inner intentionality, something more than an action or viewpoint; the state or quality of being directed. I tried to probe intentionality as the interior life of the prophet but may have failed. It seems that even when negotiating the prophetic, intentionality is crucial. Was I unable to focus on intention, so important in theory, because I thought it had to be bracketed in our complex world?

As the 2016 American presidential election debacle unfolded, the neoliberal Hillary Clinton took a disastrous fall, and Donald Trump's presidency became a dystopic reality, finding a consequential dissident voice became more urgent. After the Obama years, so different in tone, yet so deficient in many policy areas, it became clear that the American political system is too limited to initiate and sustain the foundational change America and the world needs so urgently. The rise of China, with the internal mass dislocation and exploitation involved, is more of the same, though it comes at a climate time when the margin for error is thin, if such a margin exists any longer. Then there was Israel in 2018, turning away Gaza's Great March of Return, with Israeli snipers firing inside Gaza's borders, killing and maiming. There is be more to come.

Perhaps the world is always in a mess and we, through scientific and technological sophistication, are more aware of it now.

Finding Our Voice

Regardless, the world is on the verge of catastrophe. Holding off the final ecological catastrophe is the task of Aaron's generation.

The conference I spoke at in Houston was largely made up of African American pastors. I was part of a keynote team, paired with with a Palestinian Christian, Reverend Mitri Raheb. The conference was a progressive and celebratory gathering on most counts, but the shadows over the Black community were clearly present. The despair and hope of the Black community was on full display. Front and center was the failing, still lively, prophetic.

I had just returned from a month of teaching in the Philippines where I encountered a similar despair and hope. After a few weeks in Manila, I began to think of the Philippines as a still colonial space struggling to find its true independence. Searching for a subtitle for the diary of my travels, I thought of Langston Hughes, the great African American poet, and his classic poem, "Dream Deferred." Surely, the Philippines, with its wealth of beauty and talent, is a land of dreams deferred. Under its then newly elected president, Rodrigo Duterte, with his extrajudicial killings and glorification of rape, again following Hughes's poem, was the Philippines about to explode?

The Black community in America, on the edge once again, the Jewish community with its raging civil war around the question of Israel and the Palestinians, a Jew, having just returned from the Philippines, with a Palestinian, addressing a Black audience, a world of pain, struggle and hope was all right there. Palestinians have been denied their freedom, their dream. Yet it is true as well, that Jews, though realizing freedom after the Holocaust, have entered a new form of slavery. As Jews, we are enslaved to our own power. Ironically, our liberation, our Jewish dream, is being deferred by oppressing another people.

As I rose to speak in Houston, as I readied to speak Aaron's words, I realized the prophet-sharing I had written about—Jew, Palestinian, Filipino, Black—had already arrived. The question remained: Where does the shared prophetic lead us?

So after arriving, since the road ahead is unclear, do we as individuals and communities, have to backtrack, turn around,

Epilogue

so as to recoup depth and sustenance? Is backtracking a retreat? Looking out at the mostly African American audience and aside to my Palestinian colleague, the interplay of solitude and solidarity returned in a somewhat different way than I had previously experienced it. Perhaps I was simply absorbing the difference between thinking about the prophetic and performing it.

The prophetic is always entangled in thought and action; solitude and solidarity have their independent say. Yet, when both are involved, moving in tandem, the particularity of each is preserved and enhanced. The universality of our particularity expands. Enhanced and expanded, the individual and the community grows in depth and consideration. Humility is the path. Our determination remains.

Does our voice—do our voices—create light in the darkness where light is absent or simply amplify what is already present? Perhaps our voice—our voices—exist within Aaron's interpretive framework, one that exists already and begins existence anew each time we give voice to what we see and experience.

Our determination comes and goes. Our needs and desires, life itself, contributes to and interrupts our intentions. Yet the "tools" we have been given—from "which I may now seek an intentional orientation toward myself; toward various communities, my own included; toward others; toward the Other; toward the divine; toward the world"—remain. Our tools direct us, if we maintain our directedness to a way of life "toward which to strive."

Aaron's focus on a way of life resonates deeply here. An intentional way of life doesn't simply arrive. An intentional way of life isn't here as a given. We must continually strive toward the prophetic.

Striving toward the prophetic, the road ahead is difficult. Yet finding, maintaining, and expanding our voice is an intention itself. Rather than success, our witness may be that intention. Intention being the watchword, success being desired but not mandated, we are free to continue on the prophetic path with or without success. In the long run of life this may be what fidelity in history is all about.

Finding Our Voice

Our voice, honed in action, is our fidelity. It is this fidelity that we pass on to our children. What Aaron taught me—what our children teach us—is that the fidelity we live is the fidelity we bequeath. Finding our voice, we continue on.

www.ingramcontent.com/pod-product-compliance
Lightning Source LLC
Chambersburg PA
CBHW020854160426
43192CB00007B/923